UAE DIVING

there's more to life...
askexplorer.com

UAE Diving 2014/4th Edition
First Published 2001
2nd (Revised) Edition 2002
3rd (Revised) Edition 2006
4th Edition 2014 ISBN 978-9948-22-283-5

Front Cover Photograph – Carole Harris

Explorer Publishing & Distribution
PO Box 34275, Dubai
United Arab Emirates
Phone +971 (0)4 340 8805
Fax +971 (0)4 340 8806
Email info@askexplorer.com
Web askexplorer.com

WELCOME...

Congratulations – you hold in your hands the best dive buddy yet! This fourth edition of *UAE Diving* blends decades of local diving experience thanks to several divers and dive schools in the UAE who have offered their knowledge and insight. The book also sports a fresh new look, making it easier to use. We've removed a couple of sites that are no longer popular due to low visibility, but we've also added a total of 13 new sites – including the newest wreck on the west coast, the *Victoria Star*. The good news is that some of the dives we previously listed as affected by construction are now back on the scene too.

There are some stunning new photos provided by local talented divers who know the sites intimately, and we've updated all the maps and dive site diagrams where necessary.

The Further Info section contains details about activities that go hand-in-hand with diving, such as snorkelling and dhow or yacht charters; essential first aid knowledge; the lowdown on all aspects of diving and a directory of dive operators and accommodation options to assist you in planning your next dive trip. And we've provided up-to-date information on border crossings to Oman.

While we urge you to get out there and enjoy the diving, just remember that it can be a long journey back to shore and a recompression chamber, so do take care and check our updated information on where to find diving doctors and recompression chambers.

If you have any comments about the book, or any pearls of diving information, we would be very happy to hear from you. Leave a comment on our facebook page (facebook.com/askexplorer) or mail us at info@askexplorer.com.

We hope you enjoy the fine diving in the UAE and Musandam. We certainly enjoyed putting the information together for you! See you under the water.

The Explorer Team

there's more to life...
ask**explorer**.com

The Al Boom Diving Advantage

- **Dedicated Call Center** for centralised bookings. Contact 04 3422993 / abdiving@emirates.net.ae
- **Open 365 days a year**
- You'll find Al Boom Diving at the following.

Prime Locations: Atlantis, the Palm; Al Wasl Rd, Jumeriah; Al Quoz close to Mall of the Emirates; Dubai Aquarium and Underwater Zoo; Le Meriden Al Aqah Beach Resort and Spa.

- **Beginners and experienced divers welcome** from Sorkeling trips and Discover Scuba Dives to PADI Dive Master and Instructor Courses. Would you like to experience breathing underwater without getting your hair wet? Ask about our unique Shark Walker Experience.
- **Variety** Al Boom Diving has something for everyone, shallow or deep; from the reefs and wrecks of the Arabian Sea on the East Coast; Fjords of the Musandam by traditional Dhow; Wrecks and World Islands off Dubai's Coast; Aquaventure Waterpark's Shark Lagoon in Atlantis, The Palm with 14 species of sharks and stingrays; to the 10-million litre tank and home to the largest collection of Sand Tiger sharks in the world in Dubai Mall's Dubai Aquarium and Underwater Zoo.
- **Onsite training pools and classrooms** at three of our Dive Centers.
- **UAE's largest fleet of dive boats**
- **UAE's largest Team of PADI professionals**
- **Aqua Lung** – Aqua Lung is the name that first introduced the world to Scuba diving more than 60 years ago when Jacques-Yves Cousteau and Émile Gagnan developed the first "Aqua-Lung." As the U.A.E's exclusive Distributor , Al Boom Diving uses. Aqua Lung equipment across all of our dive centers.
- **Dive Shops** Al Boom Diving is a GCC wide Distributor for top brands such as Aqua Lung, Apeks, Aqua Sphere, Cressi, Omer, Innovative Scuba, Ikelite and much, much more. Our own four dive shops are packed full of the latest scuba, free diving, snorkeling and swimming equipment and you'll also find our products in many of the leading sports stores across the GCC.
- **Air Quality** – we are a Dealer and Service Center for Bauer Air Compressors. All of our Dive Centers have air fill facilities on site. Nitrox and mixed gas is available on request.
- **Workshop** Our well renowned scuba workshop in Al Quoz is the only facility of its kind in the UAE ensuring that we have the aftersales capability to back up the brands which we represent and service our rental equipment to the manufacturer's standards. The workshop also caters to most well-known scuba brands.
- **DAN Insurance** (Divers Alert Network, Europe). DAN Short Term Insurance is included in the price of our Open Water Course. We recommend that certified divers have their own dive insurance however DAN day-dive Insurance is available upon request at the time of booking your dive.

www.alboomdiving.com

CONTENTS

CONTRIBUTORS

Thanks to these divers, we have the latest dive site info

Christophe Chellapermal

Chris loved the water since he was a child, and became a PADI Scuba Instructor in 1998. He also loves photography, and has provided several superb shots for this guide as well as updates on several dive sites. Founder and owner of Nomad Ocean Adventures, he does all he can to involve Nomad with environmental conservation.

Neil Murphy

Neil is General Manager for Sheesa Beach Travel and Tourism, which he set up in 2010. He's an ex-commercial diver who ventured into recreational dive management in 2004, and has been a PADI professional since 2000. Neil is an adventurous diver and gave us some great info about some of the more exciting dives in Musandam.

Matt Christensen

Matt has been diving for five years and is a PADI IDC Staff Instructor. He now works as Lead Instructor for Divers Down. His favourite east coast dive spots are Inchcape 1 and Three Rocks because of their range of marine life. Divers Down offers pleasure diving and PADI courses, and is well known for its outstanding training.

Kathleen Russell

In her 18 years of diving, Kathleen has gained more diving certifications than we have space to list! She owns Al Mahara Diving Center and Desert Islands Watersports Center in Abu Dhabi and Ruwais, and is committed to promoting dive safety, and the preservation and conservation of the marine environment.

Ken Atkinson

Ken has been diving for more than 25 years and has 5,000+ dives under his belt. He's the owner and manager of Prodive Middle East, and caters for recreational and technical divers. Prodive can tailor make specific dive programmes for individuals, groups and corporate clients, and they offer chocolate brownies on their dive trips!

Jason Sockett

Jason has been teaching scuba diving in the UAE and Oman for 18 years. A PADI Course Director and owner of The Dive Centre, he is happiest when he is diving and teaching people to dive; he loves passing on his passion for the underwater world. He has provided some top tips for the wreck dives on the west coast.

Carole Harris

Carole completed her first dive course in the UAE in 1986. She then obtained her BSAC Advanced Instructor and PADI Divemaster shortly afterwards. She's clocked up more than 3,000 dives, and the expertise that she contributed to the first edition of this book, still forms the base of the newer edition today.

Tony Schroder

Tony's first diving experience was with the Jebel Ali BSAC 916 club in 1988. From there he gained his BSAC First Class Diver and Advanced Instructor certificates. During his 20 years in the UAE, Tony collected valuable information about the many wreck sites, which we have built upon in this latest version of the book.

THROUGH THE LENS

Many thanks to Abdullah Al Meheiri and Shamsa Al Hameli for images of Abu Dhabi dive sites; and Nomad Ocean Adventures who provided photos taken by Francis Leguen, which feature throughout the book. For a full list of all contributors, see p.192.

UAE DIVE SITES

This map is not an authority on international boundaries

DIVING IN THE UAE

The UAE offers diving that's really very special; the lower Arabian Gulf and the Gulf of Oman will satisfy all tastes and levels of experience for divers and snorkellers alike. You can choose from over 30 wrecks in relatively shallow water, tropical coral reefs and dramatic coastlines that are virtually undived. And these are bathed in warm water all year round.

Water temperatures range from a cooler 20°C in January to a warmer 35°C in July and August. Although the land temperatures can be in the high 40s in the summer months, it is rarely too hot when out at sea or dipping into the water. Rain usually falls in the early months of the year, January – March, but it is infrequent and never lasts for long.

Areas to Dive

For the purposes of this book we've divided the region into three main areas; the west coast (lower Arabian Gulf, including Dubai and Abu Dhabi), Musandam, and the east coast (on the Gulf of Oman and the Indian Ocean side of the UAE peninsula).

Modern highways connect the coasts of the UAE. From the northern emirates, the journey from the west to the east coast is a two-hour drive, passing through rolling sand dunes, gravel plains and oasis towns, before crossing the rugged western Hajar Mountains and down to the palm-covered coastal strip of the east coast. Development here is not as advanced as elsewhere in the UAE, offering only a sprinkling of hotels and holiday resorts.

In sharp contrast, the west coast has seen a huge amount of development in the last 25 years, especially in Abu Dhabi and Dubai. Numerous hotels, including plenty of a luxury five-star standard, offer all the facilities a tourist can reasonably expect, and much more.

The weather on the east coast can be very different to that in the west of the country. In the Gulf of Oman it is slightly cooler in the summer and there may occasionally be rain in late July and August. The weather will often be calm on this coast, while the west coast is being buffeted by a 'shamal' (moderate northerly winds). If your dive on one coast is cancelled because of rough seas or high winds, the weather will probably be fine on the other coast.

Musandam is the area to the north of the UAE at the very tip of the peninsula, and

is actually part of the Sultanate of Oman. This mountainous region is very beautiful and virtually undeveloped. Its remoteness and lack of access means it is one of the least explored diving areas in the world.

Only one paved road runs north from Ras Al Khaimah in the UAE, to Khasab, capital of Musandam, and many of the small fishing villages along the coast are only accessible by boat or off-road tracks. The only hotels are located in Khasab.

Diving

There are many excellent diving centres and clubs operating here that will help you enjoy the region's wonderful diving. For the *UAE Diving* guidebook we have covered as many dive sites as possible with the aim of giving a good representation of the best known and most popular locations. Since many visitors to the UAE are based in Dubai, we have included a large number of west coast dive sites.

Only a few dive sites are safely accessible from the shore, so plan on using a boat. If you have your own boat, there are many slipways available and we have included maps and GPS coordinates of the best ones. There are also several first-class marinas where you can permanently moor your boat (for a fee).

Diver Certification

If you are a certified diver, always remember to pack your certification card – without it no dive organisation in the UAE will allow you to dive.

Learning to dive or advancing your existing qualifications with an internationally recognised organisation is very easy to do in the UAE. This can be arranged through one of the many dive centres. Refer to the Dive Directory (p.184) for contact information of dive centres on the east and west coasts.

Levels of Experience

The dive sites described in this book are chosen to suit all levels of diving experience. Energy Determination and Musandam are more challenging and require additional precautions to be safely dived. They are recommended only for more experienced divers. Ines is for qualified technical divers only. For all the other dive sites described, we advise you to take the usual precautions and assess conditions at the time of your dive.

TAKE CARE

As with all advice, comments, opinions, directions and suggestions, make sure that you first evaluate the information for yourself – use your common sense, know your limits and dive with caution.

We strongly recommend that you have completed the necessary training before attempting a dive. The minimum qualification you should have is Open Water Diver, which allows you to dive to 18m. The advanced courses that allow you to specialise in wreck, navigation or other skills will make more sites available to you and increase your enjoyment of the sport.

Explorer Group Ltd, Explorer Publishing, accepts no responsibility for any accidents, injuries, loss, inconvenience, disasters or damage to persons or property that may occur while you are out and about or using this guidebook. The fact that a site is mentioned does not necessarily mean that it is always diveable or safe.

Ultimately you are responsible for determining your own limitations based on the conditions you encounter.

HOW TO SELECT A DIVE

1 By name

If you know the name of a dive you'd like to look up, look at the index at the back of the book. As many dives also have alternatives to the most commonly used names, we've listed the dives by all known names.

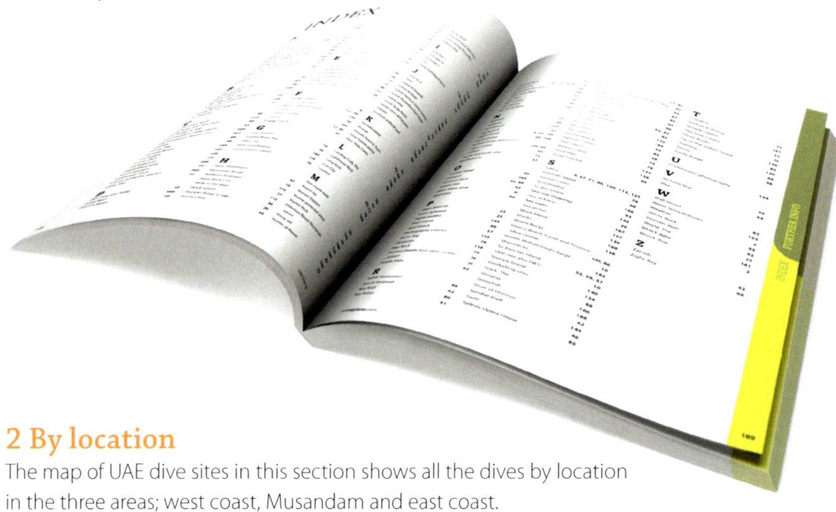

2 By location

The map of UAE dive sites in this section shows all the dives by location in the three areas; west coast, Musandam and east coast.

3 By area

Each of the three individual sections begins with an overview map that shows the location of all the dives featured in that area.

4 By attributes

The Dive Overview Table on p.XVIII gives you an at-a-glance look at the attributes of each dive. The depth of the site is listed along with the distance of the site from shore (where multiple harbours have been given we've chosen the harbour closest to the site). Separate columns for different types of dives show whether you can explore a reef or wreck, or if it is a wall or drift dive. There are also columns to show whether you can dive this site at night or snorkel there. In addition, this table lists the dives we believe are the 'must dos' during your time in the UAE.

THE ANATOMY OF A DIVE

Each individual site starts with a brief description of the dive, key information about the site, as well as a diagram showing the aspect of the wreck or reef with a north orientation arrow. This means that at a glance you'll be able to see the depth of the dive, any other names it may be known by, GPS coordinates for the location, distances from commonly used harbours for the dive and to or from other sites (for maps of the locations of all harbours, see p.173), and also whether the site is suitable for night dives and snorkelling. It makes dive planning a cinch.

The text for the dive starts with a general introduction to the dive, with either a history of the wreck or a general

1 DIVE 27

2 THE LANDING CRAFT

3

4 GPS
N26°12'40.0"
E56°17'05.1"

5 **Depth:** 10m | **Snorkelling:** | **Night dive:** Yes

6 **Distance from harbours:**
Khasab Harbour 3.5nm @ 079°

7 A sheltered site that offers divers a chance to practise their wreck penetration skills.

8

This was a landing craft that specialised in carrying water to the villages that weren't able to receive water by road. The vessel was one of a fleet of three boats, each named after one of the villages they frequented with their essential load.

The hull of The Musandam split with age, and it was decided that the vessel would be decommissioned. There was also a light aircraft that had been at Khasab Airport for about two years and the decision was made to load the plane onto the landing craft and take them out to sea to be sunk.

Diving

This small vessel sits upright and intact on the seabed at just 10m, with its bow facing 20°. The Musandam has a well-preserved and undamaged wheelhouse, which is surprising given that it's only 3-4m from the surface, and you can swim in and out of it easily. On a past dive, a prankster placed the loo on top of the wheelhouse.

You will be able to see the engine room through gaps in the deck, but it's a very tight squeeze and entry is certainly not to be attempted without adequate training.

Another interesting feature is the

70 UAE Diving

1 Number of dive
2 Name of dive
3 QR code. Scan to access location map
4 GPS coordinates
5 Key features
6 Distance from harbours
7 Brief description
8 Diagram of dive site

NEW DIGITAL IMAGES

Thanks to talented photographers (see the Contributors' page for details), we've added excellent close-up pictures of colourful marine life along the UAE's coasts. We're sure the photos will entice you to dive.

description of the site and local area. It then goes into detail regarding the diving, along with specific information on snorkelling if applicable, and marine life. If the dive is a wreck dive, further details of the vessel can be found on the second page in the Wreck Data info box. This includes type of vessel, size, date sunk and any cargo sunk with the vessel. For more information on wreck data, refer to Shipping Weights and Measures on p.180. For this edition of the guide we've added QR codes; simply scan them with your mobile device and you'll see a map of the dive location instantly.

Scan the QR code with a smartphone for a map of the dive site

aeroplane laid out on the deck with its wings alongside. You can see the propellers and the cockpit area with petrol tanks underneath what's left of the seats. At the front of the vessel is the landing deck which seems to attract a plethora of fish life. You can also find small bits and pieces of debris and tyres strewn about the wreckage.

After looking for shrimps, crabs and blennies in all the nooks and crannies on the wreck, take a swim over to the edge of the reef and look in the staghorn corals. You're likely to find a citron goby city in every coral you peer into.

This is an ideal beginners' site on the edge of a protected bay with the rocky shoreline close by. It's only 15 minutes to the harbour, making it an easy night dive destination.

Snorkelling

Snorkellers will enjoy this site too, as it's relatively shallow and it's possible to see the wreckage from the surface most of the time.

Marine Life

As the wreck has been here for several years, you'll see many shells and a variety of hard corals on it; primarily brain and staghorn corals encrusted around anything they can find, such as the wreck's surfaces, along ropes, and clinging to the metal...

As Khasab isn't dived as much as other UAE sites, the fish appear to be quite unconcerned about divers and will swim almost into your face and regulator.

Yellow snappers are always in abundance, especially in and around the landing ramp area. You're also likely to spot a couple of clownfish and anemone colonies.

Safety

This is a good site for students thanks to its protected position. You still need to take the precautions you'd usually take when diving a wreck though, and watch that you and your equipment are not caught or cut on the rusty wreckage. It's also important that you wear protective

9

Wreck register: Not charted
Name: The Musandam
Nationality: Unknown
Year built: Unknown
Type: Landing craft
Tonnage: Unknown
Dimensions: L: 35m, B: 7m, D: 3m
Cargo: None
Date sunk: 1990

MUSANDAM

THE LANDING CRAFT

WARNING
Do not attempt to enter the engine room without adequate training. There's also a lot of rubbish in the form of rusted cans and broken glass lying around here.

Diver in the wheelhouse

askexplorer.com 71

9 Wreck data
10 Section name
11 Dive name

SNORKELLING OPTIONS

You don't have to be a scuba diver to appreciate this book; snorkellers will find tons of interesting sites listed too. There's lots to see from the surface, and if you want to learn to duck dive, turn to the Further Info section.

OVERVIEW TABLE

Dive	Name	Page	Depth (m)	Distance (nm)	Drift	Reef	Wall	Wreck	Snorkelling	Night
WEST COAST										
1	Anchor Barge	6	23	18.6				✓		✓
2	Barracuda Barge	8	18	4				✓	✓	
3	DB1/SMB	10	25	12				✓		
4	Energy Determination ★	14	80+	35				✓		
5	Hammour Barge	18	15	14.9				✓		✓
6	Hopper Barge 6	20	23	18.7				✓		✓
7	Jaramac V	22	23	10.4				✓		
8	Jasim	26	27	28.7				✓		✓
9	Jazirat Sir Bu Na'air	28	36	43.5	✓	✓			✓	✓
10	Lion City	30	30	27				✓		✓
11	Mariam Express ★	32	21	14.7				✓		
12	MV Dara	34	18	5.8				✓		✓
13	MV Hannan	36	20	33				✓		
14	MV Ludwig ★	38	27	26				✓		✓
15	Nasteran	40	23	5.6				✓		✓
16	Neptune 6	42	23	18.7				✓		✓
17	Swift	46	38	51.1				✓		
18	Turtle Barge	48	8	5.2				✓	✓	✓
19	Victoria Star	50	22	13.23				✓		✓
20	Zainab ★	52	29	18.1				✓		✓
21	Al Dhabiyah Coral Garden	55	10	18.72		✓				
22	Car Cemetery	55	14-16	101.4						
23	Gasha Buoy Rig	56	14-19	72.35						
24	Hook Island	56	15	91.5		✓				
25	Pearl Wreck	57	12	99.1				✓		
MUSANDAM										
26	The Caves	68	10-18	10.5			✓		✓	✓
27	The Landing Craft	70	10	3.5					✓	✓
28	Lima Rock ★	72	12-60	20.3	✓	✓	✓		✓	✓
29	Bu Rashid	75	6-40+	20.3	✓	✓	✓	✓		
30	Ennerdale Rock	75	16-50+	25.9	✓	✓	✓			
31	Fanaku Island	76	6-50+	24	✓	✓	✓			
32	Great Quion Island	76	16-50+	23.8	✓	✓	✓			
33	Hard Rock Cafe ★	77	6-20+	39.5	✓	✓	✓	✓	✓	
34	Jazirat Al Khayl	77	16-40+	18.3	✓	✓	✓			
35	Jazirat Hamra &	78	6-30	35.3		✓	✓			
36	Jazirat Sawda	78	6-30+	35.7		✓	✓			
37	Jazirat Musandam East Head	78	6-50+	25.1	✓	✓	✓			

★ Must do

Dive	Name	Page	Depth (m)	Distance (nm)	Drift	Reef	Wall	Wreck	Snorkelling	Night
38	Jazirat Umm Al Fayyarin	79	6-50+	39.8	✓	✓	✓			
39	Kachalu Island	79	6-40+	22.5	✓	✓	✓			
40	Mushroom Rock	80	5-25	34.4	✓	✓	✓			
41	Ras Alull	80	5-25	33.6	✓	✓	✓			
42	Ras Arous	81	5-25	34.1		✓				✓
43	Ras Bashin	81	4-25	37.7	✓	✓				
44	Ras Dillah	82	6-40+	40.2	✓	✓	✓			
45	Ras Dillah Ghubbat Ash Shabus Bay	82	6-30+	39.4		✓	✓			
46	Ras Khaysah South	83	10-35	34.1	✓	✓	✓			
47	Ras Kaysah North	83	20-25	22.2	✓	✓	✓			
48	Ras Musandam	83	6-50+	22.6	✓	✓	✓			
49	Ras Qabr Al Hindi	83	6m-30+	29.3	✓	✓				
50	Ras Samid	84	5-15	47.7		✓				
51	Ras Sarkan	84	6-50+	42.2	✓	✓	✓	✓		
52	Ruqq Suwayk	85	6-50+	19.6		✓	✓	✓		
53	White Rock	85	6-50+	34.5	✓	✓	✓			
54	Octopus Rock ★	88	5-20	23	✓	✓	✓		✓	✓
55	Pearl Island	90	5-12	20.6	✓	✓	✓		✓	✓
56	Ras Hamra	92	5-16	20.4	✓	✓	✓		✓	✓
57	Ras Lima	94	5-45	18.8	✓	✓	✓		✓	✓
58	Ras Marovi	96	6-35	21	✓	✓	✓		✓	✓

EAST COAST

Dive	Name	Page	Depth (m)	Distance (nm)	Drift	Reef	Wall	Wreck	Snorkelling	Night
59	Anemone Gardens ★	102	20	0.9		✓			✓	✓
60	Car Cemetery	104	18	1.6				✓		✓
61	Coral Gardens ★	106	26	1.1		✓				✓
62	Deep Reef ★	108	30	4.53	✓	✓				✓
63	Dibba Island ★	110	16	5.2		✓			✓	✓
64	Hole in the Wall	112	15	4.53		✓			✓	✓
65	Inchcape 1	114	32	4.53				✓		✓
66	Inchcape 2 ★	118	22	1.8				✓		✓
67	Inchcape 10	124	24	1.53				✓		✓
68	Ines	126	72	6.2				✓		
69	Martini Rock ★	128	3-22	2		✓	✓		✓	✓
70	Murbah Reef	130	5-14	8.2		✓			✓	✓
71	Ras Qidfa	132	8	2.7		✓	✓		✓	✓
72	Refinery Reef	134	28	10.8		✓				✓
73	Shark Island	136	16	0.8		✓	✓		✓	✓
74	Sharm Rocks	138	14	5.3		✓	✓		✓	✓
75	Snoopy Island	140	8	5.5		✓	✓		✓	✓

WEST COAST

WEST COAST:

A WRECK DIVER'S PARADISE

Wreck divers will revel in what the west coast has to offer, with some of the wrecks here dating back to the early 60s. All the sites can only be accessed by boat, but the trip is generally worthwhile as the wrecks attract a plethora of marine life.

At 984km long, the Arabian Gulf is a shallow extension of the Indian Ocean, and offers a sandy, almost flat, featureless seabed with a few isolated coral reefs. Its narrowest point is at the Strait of Hormuz (the northern tip of the peninsula), where it is 56km wide. The average depth along the UAE coast is 30m, increasing to over 100m through the Strait of Hormuz.

The tidal movement is slight, with the currents only becoming stronger during spring tides and around the full moon. With a few exceptions, the currents have little effect on most of the dives. Visibility ranges between five and 15m, although there are exceptional days when it reaches 20m plus. Most of the wrecks are within a 30 minute boat journey of the shore.

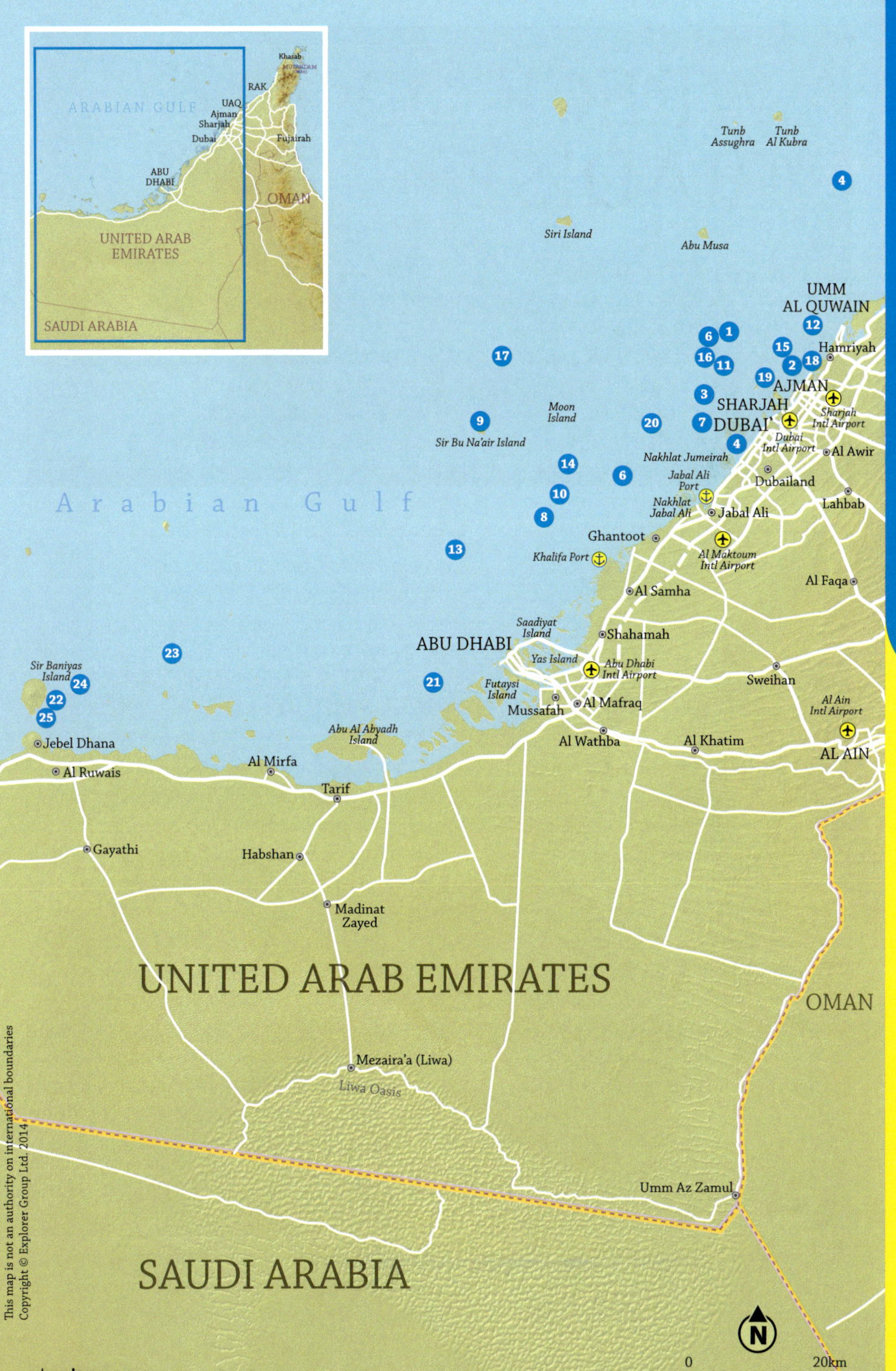
ARABIAN GULF
RAK
UAQ
Ajman
Sharjah
Dubai
Fujairah
ABU DHABI
OMAN
UNITED ARAB EMIRATES
SAUDI ARABIA
Tunb Assughra
Tunb Al Kubra
Siri Island
Abu Musa
UMM AL QUWAIN
Hamriyah
AJMAN
SHARJAH
DUBAI
Sharjah Intl Airport
Dubai Intl Airport
Al Awir
Moon Island
Sir Bu Na'air Island
Nakhlat Jumeirah
Jabal Ali Port
Dubailand
Lahbab
Nakhlat Jabal Ali
Jabal Ali
Arabian Gulf
Ghantoot
Al Maktoum Intl Airport
Khalifa Port
Al Faqa
Al Samha
Saadiyat Island
Shahamah
ABU DHABI
Yas Island
Abu Dhabi Intl Airport
Sweihan
Sir Baniyas Island
Futaysi Island
Al Mafraq
Mussafah
Al Ain Intl Airport
Abu Al Abyadh Island
Al Wathba
Al Khatim
AL AIN
Jebel Dhana
Al Mirfa
Al Ruwais
Tarif
Gayathi
Habshan
Madinat Zayed
UNITED ARAB EMIRATES
OMAN
Mezaira'a (Liwa)
Liwa Oasis
Umm Az Zamul
SAUDI ARABIA
N
0
20km

Night Diving

Night diving on the west coast is spectacular; dive with a powerful light at night to light up the colours, and be amazed. The wrecks, which appear orange and muddy brown during the day, turn into rainbows of colour at night and a whole new set of marine residents appear to feed and forage on and around them.

The wrecks offer such a small area of sanctuary for the fish that they have to hide in every available hole, crevice and corner. As a diver this means that you can get very close to a wide variety of resting fish.

At night, sites such as Nasteran are always special and memorable. With the exception of the Jasim, Lion City and MV Ludwig, we have dived all the sites covered in this book at night, even the Energy Determination, which is a real thrill full of life.

A word of caution when returning from the more distant sites, especially at night when everyone wants to get home as quickly as possible. Beware, as running into unmarked fishing nets is a very real danger. The nets can jam around the propellers, immobilising the boat. There's also sometimes the odd piece of semi-submerged debris drifting about, which is difficult to spot, particularly at night, which is difficult to spot, particularly at night, and easily run into.

DIVER SAFETY

To ensure that your wreck dives safe and enjoyable, keep the following points in mind:

- Wear protective clothing. The wreck's surface may be covered with stinging hydrocorals and protruding pieces of jagged metal.
- Do not enter a wreck without appropriate training.
- If it's your first time on a site and you don't have a dive guide, do not enter the wreck unless a large exit point is visible on the other side.
- Be extra careful if you're diving a wreck after a storm; it may have become unstable or fragile.
- If you intend to penetrate a wreck, take along a rope or guideline that you can tie to the outside of the structure, and use to help you find your way out.
- Take a torch or flashlight.
- Once you swim inside the wreck be cautious, as wrecks tend to silt up quickly. By controlling your finning techniques you'll minimise the chance of stirring the silt up and clouding the visibility.

DIVE 1

ANCHOR BARGE

GPS
N25°30'47.6"
E55°04'35.7"

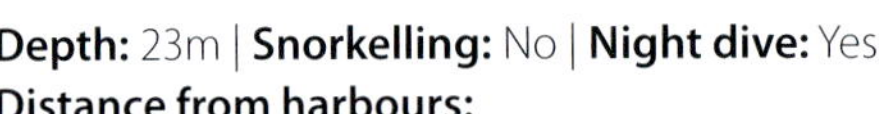

Depth: 23m | **Snorkelling:** No | **Night dive:** Yes
Distance from harbours:
Abu Dhabi Club 70.6nm @ 032°; DIMC 25.4nm @ 350°; Dubai Creek 18.6nm @ 319°
Distance from other dive sites:
HB6 (p.20) 0.6nm @ 059°
Neptune 6 (p.42) 0.7nm @ 055°

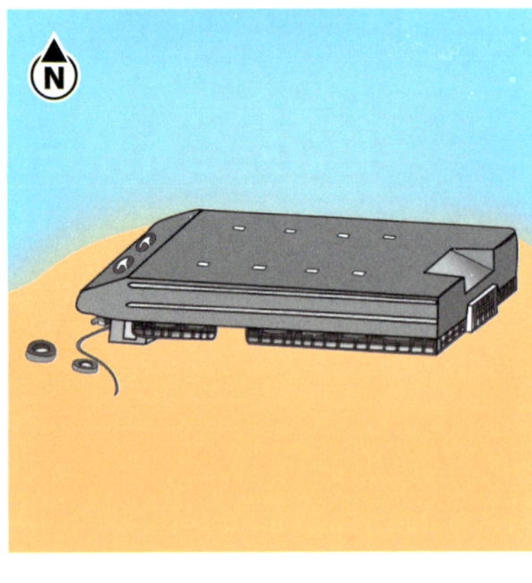

A site well worth exploring and a good place to watch the cuttlefish swim by.

Sunk by the White Sea Shipping Company in 1998 to form an artificial reef, the anchor barge is a large upsidedown wreck. She rests on her forward machinery cabin in 23m of water, and the roomy open area between her deck and the seabed means that there's plenty of hiding space for sea creatures.

The cabin contains anchor winches and the cargo and ballast transfer pumps, with her bulk being supported by the cabin and deck equipment. The wreck lies on a ridge of rock a metre high. Not all operators dive this wreck, due to its distance.

Diving

This is one of the few dive sites in the Gulf where the seabed has some features that are worth exploring. You should take a powerful torch to search under the hull of the barge. Make sure you look up at whatever has taken up residence on the overhead deck.

As the vessel is rectangular and slab-sided and the currents can be quite strong on this site, it can sometimes be rather difficult to anchor here.

But the reward is that, once you're in the water, there's an abundance of marine life.

Anchor Barge being sunk

Marine Life

Scallops, oysters and small clumps of black sea squirts have taken hold of the wreck, along with hydrocorals. On the surrounding sand and rocky bottom, flatworms (black with a colourful orange edging) abound in February and March.

You also have a good chance of seeing cuttlefish on this site. These amazing creatures have a neon-like line that runs around their mantle, and they can alter their colour and shape to blend in with their surroundings.

Wreck register: Unknown
Name: Pontoon 300 (formerly The Leena)
Nationality: Unknown
Year built: Unknown
Type: MV barge
Tonnage: 3,900 tonnes gross
Dimensions: L: 82m, B: 27m, D: 5m
Cargo: Ballast
Date sunk: April 1998

Cuttlefish

GOING ARTIFICIAL

The benefit of sinking an old vessel, or even an obsolete rig, is that it provides a habitat for hundreds of underwater species to live and feed on. This is generally a positive change, especially where the seabed is largely flat and featureless. It's no guarantee that a wreck will become a healthy and diverse reef, but the chances are that nature will snap up the opportunity.

To read an account of how a wreck is gradually transformed into a reef, turn to A Year in the Life of Inchcape 2 on p.122.

DIVE 2

BARRACUDA BARGE

GPS
N25°27'15.6"
E55°22'41.4"

Depth: 18m | **Snorkelling:** Yes | **Night dive:** No

Distance from harbours:
Ajman Creek 4nm @ 298°
DIMC 25.1nm @ 030°
Hamriya Harbour 6.3nm @ 256°
Sharjah Creek 4.6nm @ 353°

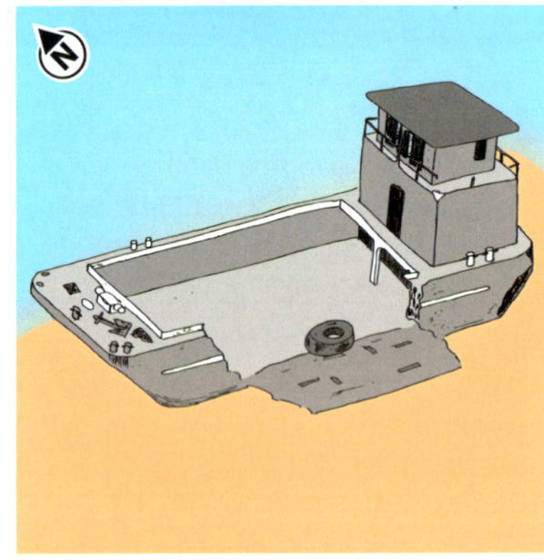

This old barge is now home to plenty of barracuda, particularly in the cooler months.

Although the circumstances of loss aren't fully known, the fact that the vessel's engine and steering gear have been removed would suggest that a local fisherman sunk this barge to form an artificial reef. In the winter of 1997, a fisherman told Blue Planet Diving about the wreck and its location.

The barge sits upright in 18m with her bow facing 340°. The seabed is flat and featureless and there are a few bits of wreckage scattered about. Unusually, for a barge, the wheelhouse and engine room are double-storeyed.

Several windows and doors give divers easy access to the interior, but when you enter the small rooms be careful not to stir up the silt, which dramatically reduces the visibility.

The top of the wheelhouse is at 10m and covered in algae and shells. You'll find small shoals of surprisingly tame fish congregating around it.

The small wreck is easily circumnavigated several times in a dive. Take your time inspecting the outside hull and look for small gobies with shrimp in their sandy homes on the seabed. Then explore the hold before you go in and out of the wheelhouse. Check out the unusual anchor still sitting on the bow.

Snorkelling

Snorkellers will enjoy this site and will see the wheelhouse easily from the surface.

Marine Life

During the winter months this wreck is surrounded by shoals of barracuda, although during the summer months they move to cooler, deeper water. Barracuda Barge is also home to the usual yellow snappers. These fish literally engulf the wreck, swimming above, around and within it, and squeezing into every available nook and cranny, no matter how small.

The cowries you'll see here are a similar rusty-brown colour to the ones found on MV Dara, which is a result of them absorbing the iron oxide from the rusting barge. The wreck is covered in orange, red, brown and black sponges, and lots of barnacles with their feathery arms that feed on small algae and other morsels. Several types of nudibranchs inhabit this wreck, their gills pulsing as they breathe (look to see if you can find their eggs in circular patterns close by). You'll also notice a white, fern-like plant; take care as these are stinging hydroids and may give you a nasty sting or rash.

Wreck register: Not charted
Name: Original name unknown
Nationality: Unknown
Year built: Unknown
Type: MV coastal barge – single screw
Tonnage: 800 tonnes gross
Dimensions: L: 30m, B: 10m, D: 4m
Cargo: None
Date sunk: Unknown

Barracuda

DIVE 3

DB1/SMB

GPS

N25°16'47.5"
E55°03'44.5"

Depth: 25m
Distance from harbours:
DIMC 12nm 337°
DOSC 10.5nm @ 306°

The Derrick Barge (or DB1) was a purpose-built towing barge, completed on 8 October, 1962. She had three decks, a helicopter pad on the stern and a 1,500 tonne American crane on the bow. DB1 is also known as Sheikh Mohammed's Barge (or SMB) as he agreed to the upkeep of the marker buoy in perpetuity.

The wreck was sunk by the UAE armed forces to form an artificial reef, along with a number of other surplus vessels and wrecks that form separate dive sites in their own right. She currently lies upside down in 23m of water on a flat, sandy bottom.

Diving

Previously affected by bad visibility due to construction, we are pleased to report that dive centres are now returning to this site.

The DB1 is one of the most interesting of the wreck dives – and it's big. It takes many dives to become familiar with the area and most people only have a clear understanding of the site when the visibility reaches 15-20m.

There are numerous holes in the wreck for the more adventurous to investigate. The DB1's hull is breaking up, and great care should be taken when exploring inside as parts of it are collapsing and there are many jagged edges.

Start on the seabed and then move up the sides of the wreck looking for nudibranchs, crabs and shrimps. This way you'll end your dive on the upturned hull at 16m. Leave enough air to do a safety stop on the anchor rope.

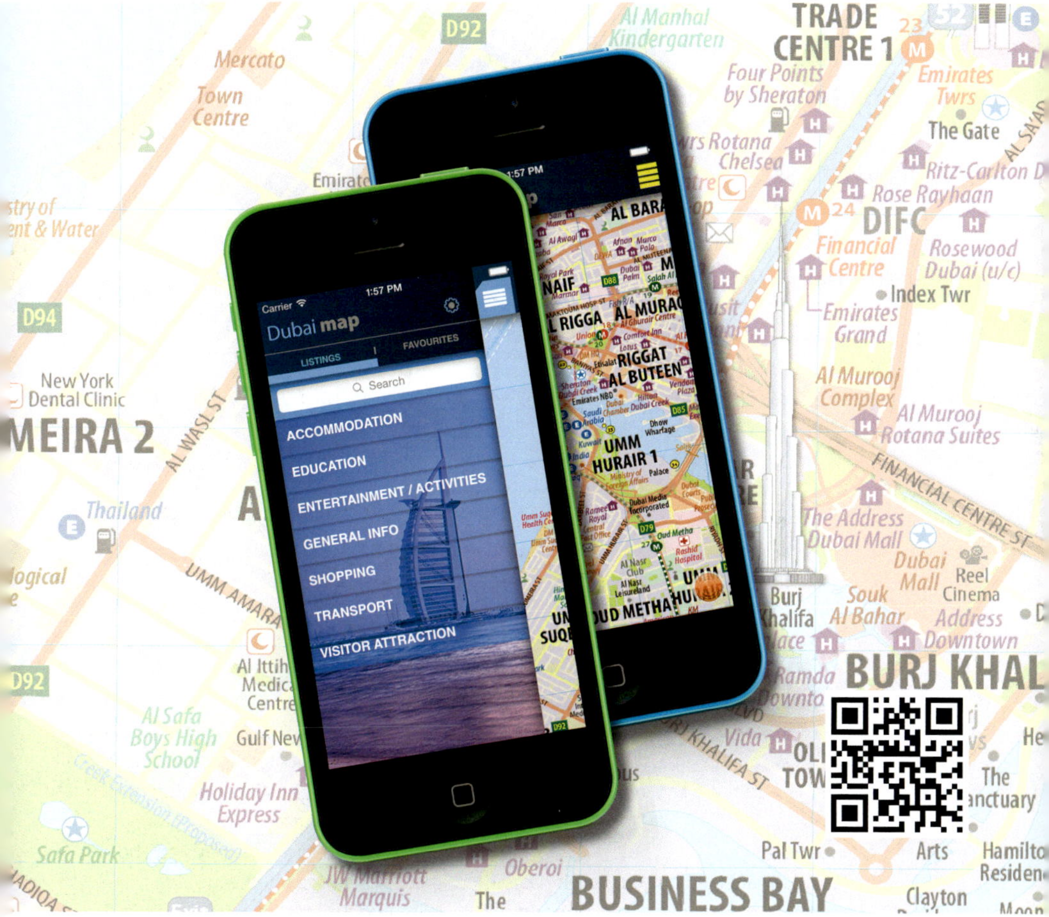

UNDERWATER ABSTRACTS

The fin detail of a scorpionfish

Daisy coral

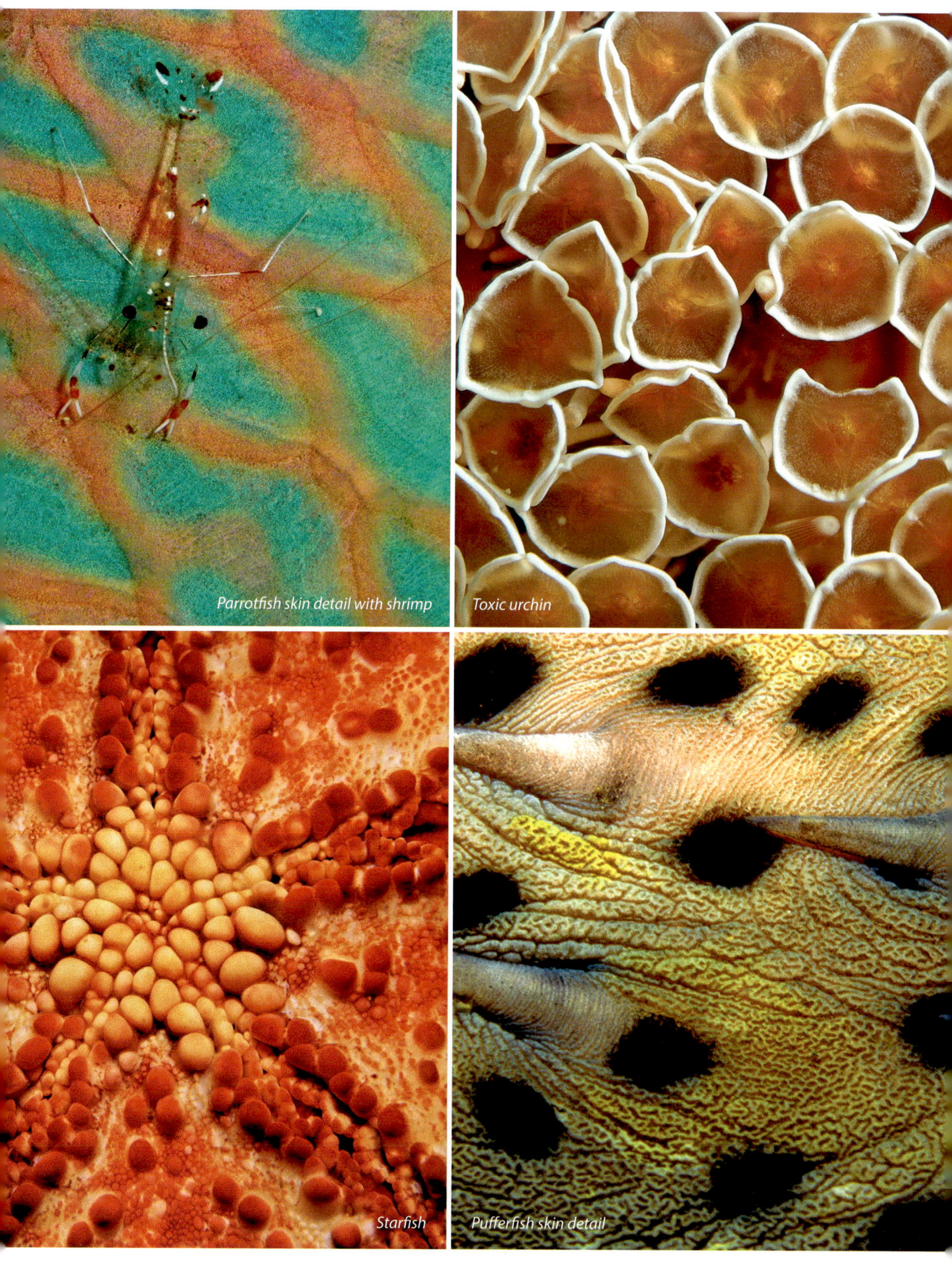

Parrotfish skin detail with shrimp

Toxic urchin

Starfish

Pufferfish skin detail

DIVE 4

ENERGY DETERMINATION

GPS
N26°04'08.1"
E55°34'04.1"

Depth: 80m+ | **Snorkelling:** No | **Night dive:** No
Distance from harbours:
DOSC 56.7nm @ 018°
Dubai Creek 49.9nm @ 016°
Hamriya Harbour 35nm @ 004°
Sharjah Creek 42.5nm @ 013°

This wreck has an interesting story behind it and plenty of scope for exploration.

The Energy Determination sailed with ballast from Bonaire, Netherlands Antilles on 5 November, 1979. She was bound for Das Island in the Gulf, where she was due to load a cargo of crude oil. However, at 1am local time on 13 December, as the Energy Determination was passing through the Strait of Hormuz, about 64km from Ras Al Khaimah, there was an enormous explosion. A fire broke out near the number 9 starboard tank, which contained 354 tons of slops. Fire and smoke quickly spread to the engine room and living quarters.

The captain decided to abandon ship and the life rafts were deployed. Of her 38 man crew, 37 were picked up from their life rafts by an Omani naval vessel that was in the area.

Meanwhile, the fiercely blazing Energy Determination, visible over 15km away and with burning fuel oil leaking from a hole in her starboard side, began to list and settle by the stern.

Salvage tugs that had raced to the scene noted that the deck and starboard side had a hole some 13m wide from the bridge house towards the bow. The

Colourful whip corals on wreck surface

Wreck register: 10830047
Name: Energy Determination
Nationality: Liberian
Year built: Unknown
Type: VLCC (very large crude carrier)
Tonnage: 321,186 DWT, 250,000 tonnes gross
Dimensions: L: 350m, B: 55m, D: 22m
Cargo: Ballast
Date sunk: 15 December, 1979

salvage crews managed to get a line on board and they towed the crippled ship to a safe position clear of the shipping lanes.

At 4.30am on 15 December, Energy Determination broke in two, 27m forward of the bridge superstructure. The stern section containing the engine room, accommodation and pump room sank east of Mina Saqr at a depth of approximately 80m. The bow section was towed towards Dubai and anchored 11km off the coast for over two years, until it was sold to South Korean shipbreakers.

She left Dubai under tow on 1 March, 1982. The insurance value of the hull and machinery was US$58 million, making her, up until December 1988, the largest total hull loss ever underwritten by Lloyd's.

Diving

Diving the Energy Determination is not for the inexperienced or faint-hearted. Great care must be taken in the preparation and planning of this dive.

Whale shark and company

Marble ray

The currents can run at over five knots, so you should plan to dive in slack water in neap tides. (Tide tables are generally only available for Port Rashid and Khor Fakkan, so some calculations must be made to determine slack water.) You should plan to arrive at the site early to allow for tidal differences in the locality.

Anchoring onto the wreck can be time consuming — due to the depth and current, the line bellies out, not allowing the anchor to reach the wreck. The preferred method is to use a redundant shot line and not to anchor. For safety, an additional cylinder and regulator should be rigged on the shot line at 10m.

The vessel's stern section rests on her port side in 80-90m of water. The wreck lies on an incline, and the depth from the surface to the top of the wreck is about 25m at the forward starboard section, descending to 60m at the stern.

The accommodation deck and machinery flat (the cabin-like structure over the engine room), are more or less intact, but the bridge is canted and partially torn off. The deck and tank directly forward of the accommodation area have been ripped out, leaving a big jagged hole that has ladders running down into the darkness. This gaping hole extends forward for about 10m to where the deck and hull remain intact. The remaining 25m of deck and hull come to an abrupt end where the bow section has broken off.

Marine Life

The forward 25m section of the hull is covered in yellow, white and red soft corals, and some lime green whip corals. Strong currents allow these corals to grow and when you swim down, their bright colours glow in the gloom.

The fish are big and tame on this site. Among other creatures, you may see large, rather frightening, but surprisingly tame marble rays, or even a whale shark. One has been photographed at close quarters on this wreck and a particularly lucky dive group were on the wreck when a whale shark party of five appeared.

Whip corals

THE OL' FLY & DIVE

Combining diving and flying is always a little risky, so you should stop diving at least 24 hours before flying to give your body time to rehydrate and degas.

Long flights should be avoided if possible and, if you do drink alcohol during the flight, you need to top up on even more water than usual to avoid becoming dehydrated.

Energy on fire!

DIVE 5

HAMMOUR BARGE

GPS

N25°04'40.5"
E54°46'06.5"

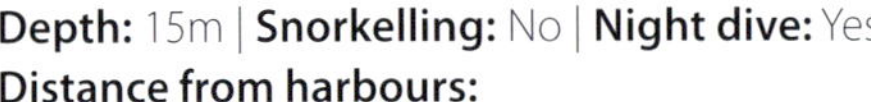

Depth: 15m | **Snorkelling:** No | **Night dive:** Yes

Distance from harbours:

Abu Dhabi Club 39.7nm @ 031°
DIMC 20.4nm @ 266°
DOSC 25.1nm @ 255°
Jebel Ali Marina 14.9nm @ 290°

Distance from other dive site:

From MV Ludwig (p.38) 11nm @ 102°

A small, accessible wreck that has been claimed by hammour as their home.

The vessel lies upright in 12-15m of water. Her hold contains a cargo of pipes that make a perfect home for hammour – which is how the site obtained its name. The wheelhouse is intact, but all the 'goodies' have been removed.

It's not known precisely when this wreck was sunk, but judging by the abundant marine growth on her, she's been resting on the seabed for at least 25 years and is home to many fish.

Diving

This is a relatively small wreck with a few scattered pieces of debris lying on the sand nearby. Our suggested dive plan is to start at the base of the vessel and to swim around it, looking on the sand and in the debris for any interesting marine life. Then carry on to inspect the hull of the barge at the point where it rests on the seabed, as this is where many of its smaller residents hide.

The small cabin is accessible and worth exploring. Make sure you take a look inside the pipes in the hold; you will always find some of the resident hammour hiding there.

Marine Life

The wreck is not often visited by divers, which means that the fish are reasonably tame. These shallow wrecks are often home to the more brightly coloured reef fish like the orange dottyback, and their less colourful cousins, the Gulf dottyback.

Keep an eye out for the several varieties of blennies to be found here. It's amazing how these colourful fish manage to squeeze into the tiniest of spaces, even trying to hide inside empty barnacle shells! They can be seen waiting near or inside their little holes with just the top of their head sticking out, ready to dart out of sight at the first sign of danger. Arabian angelfish can be seen all over the wreck, picking over the encrustations, and you might also spot some moon wrasse.

WARNING

Before attempting to dive any wreck it's strongly recommended that you receive adequate training to prepare you for diving in an overhead environment.

Wreck register: 108301272
Name: Unknown
Nationality: Unknown
Year built: Unknown
Type: Open hold barge
Tonnage: 860 tonnes gross
Dimensions: L: 60m, B: 10m, D: 5m
Cargo: Pipes
Date sunk: Unknown

Hammour

DIVE 6

HOPPER BARGE 6

Batfish

N25°30'27.9"
E55°03'58.6"

Depth: 23m | **Snorkelling:** No | **Night dive:** Yes
Distance from harbours:
DIMC 25.1nm @ 349°
DOSC 21.5nm @ 336°
Dubai Creek 18.7nm @ 317°
Distance from other dive site:
From Neptune 6 (p.42) 0.18nm @ 223°

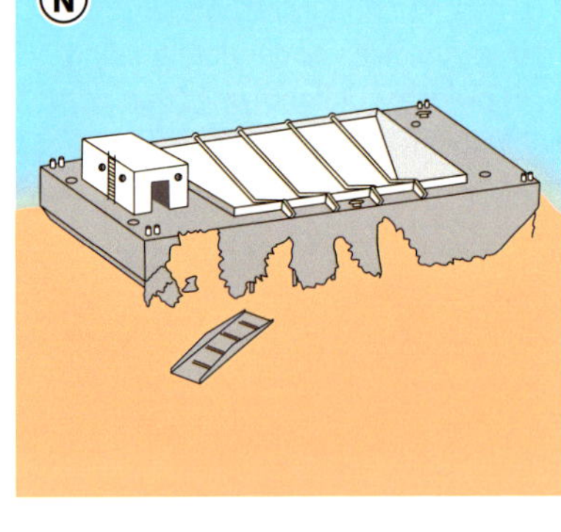

An easy wreck to navigate, with a number of interesting marine inhabitants to observe.

This is another of the wrecks that has been sunk by a local fisherman in close proximity to the Neptune 6's marker buoy (see p.42). Under international maritime law, wrecks that could be a hazard to shipping must have a marker buoy, known as a cardinal marker buoy, to indicate where there is clear water to passing vessels. However, the upkeep and maintenance of these buoys is costly (in excess of US$50,000 a year), so fishermen understandably tend to sink vessels near to existing marker buoys, rather than incur the cost of a new buoy.

The HB6 ended up here when she drifted onto the lee breakwater of Port Khalid in Sharjah during a storm on 18 February, 1982. The result was a total loss insurance claim. She was later raised, towed to her present location and sunk.

Among the sights here are the barge's drop-bottom doors, which were hydraulically operated, and the two cabins that housed the hydraulic gear on the stern. There's also a large cavity on the starboard side, which is the result of her collision with the breakwater stabits.

Diving

This is an easy wreck for navigation as HB6 sits upright in 25m, with her bows facing south at 180°, and she's situated close to the Neptune 6. Her starboard side is beginning to break up and several large holes have exposed the drop-bottom doors. The holes in the side are well worth a visit, and best explored with a torch. Entry into the machinery cabins is also possible.

Marine Life

We once found empty Cypraea pulchra cowries here when exploring one of the holes under the wreck. Known locally as 'four-eyes', these beautiful shells are light pinkish brown and have two chocolate brown blotches at each extremity.

Batfish will often follow you nearly all the way to the surface on your ascent. These large fish seem unafraid of divers; the fact that they're not targeted by fishermen could explain their friendliness.

Guitar shark

Wreck register: Not known
Name: Hopper Barge 6 (HB6)
Nationality: Panamanian registered
Year built: Unknown
Type: Dump barge
Tonnage: 1,000 tonnes gross
Dimensions: L: 48m, B: 14m, D: 5m
Cargo: None
Year sunk: Circa 1985

Blenny

DIVE 7

JARAMAC V

Juvenile fish catch a ride with a jellyfish

Depth: 23m | **Snorkelling:** No | **Night dive:** No
Distance from harbours:
DIMC 12nm @ 337°
DOSC 10.4nm @ 305°
Dubai Creek 12.7nm @ 270°

The Jaramac V forms part of the large artificial reef around the Derrik Barge (also known as DBI or Sheik Mohammed's Barge – see p.10) and is another of the sites that has now recovered from the effects of construction. She lies 200m to the northwest of DB1 but is worth a separate dive when conditions are good.

Diving

The Jaramac V sits upright on the seabed and is more or less intact. She's an easy wreck to explore and you can access the bridge, engine room and accommodation quarters without too much effort.

This small wreck is not that frequently visited, due to it previously being affected by nearby construction work. We're pleased to report that it's now thriving again, and you can even see larger marine life here. Also expect bream, batfish, barracuda, rays, groupers, cardinal fish, snappers, fusiliers, wrasse, gobies, blennies, flounders and the occasional venomous, but shy sea snake.

Wreck register: Jaramac V
Nationality: Not known
Year Built: 1963
Type: Utility Vessel
Tonnage: 118 tonnes gross
Dimensions: Not known
Date sunk: Unknown

LIFE UNDER THE PALMS

The UAE's offshore island-building projects have caused debate regarding the effects of their construction on marine life.

What the construction of the UAE's artificial islands (the Palms and The World) represents depends on your point of view: to some they're the pinnacle of progress, but to others they're an environmental disaster.

Marine experts – and divers – worry that the markedly poor visibility of the west coast's waters is the first sign that change is not necessarily for the better. While developers say that the islands have created underwater habitats, others worry about man playing at being Mother Nature.

The Price of Development

High sea temperatures and increased salinity levels in the late 1990s and early 2000s saw extensive coral bleaching in the region's reefs. While the Environment Agency Abu Dhabi reported in June 2006 that there were indications that Abu Dhabi's reefs are recovering, their environmentalists still caution the placing of additional anthropogenic (man-made) pressures on vulnerable reefs. Snorkelling off the beaches in Dubai shows that the coast's once clear waters are still cloudy in places, and divers and environmentalists have reported that some sites are no longer blessed with good visibility due to excess silt in the water. However, the good news is that several dive sites previously 'on hold' due to cloudy waters, have made a good recovery and are back on the diving

The Palm Jumeirah

Developers say that the World Islands provide a new habitat for marine life

agenda (such as Jaramac V and DB1/SMB).

Nakheel, the developers of the Palms and The World, says that the disturbance was temporary and that visibility improves within days. They argue that before the islands were built, the seabed consisted mainly of undulating, featureless sand with only a few shipwrecks and the occasional outcrop of limestone to form small reefs. The islands' rocky outer walls, they say, have created approximately 100km of reef.

New Reef Growth

Nakheel says that not only have they created new reefs, but that the developments have also given rise to a variety of habitats, including intertidal zones, seagrass meadows, protected estuarine environments and rocky reefs. Its environmental team has recorded sightings of dolphins, manta rays, trevally and sharks within Palm Jumeirah's waters.

The developer also points out that, according to marine experts, Dubai's largest coral reef has grown by more than 20% since moving to a new home at The World islands in 2008, when the company spent Dhs.36 million moving 2,200 square metres of reef more than 18km underwater to save it from the effects of infrastructure development. Six years on, the coral has expanded by more than a fifth, and now comprises 18 types of coral including new spawnings and 30 species of reef-associated fish.

As compensatory habitat, the new reefs provide more than a 10-fold increase over the area of patchy natural reef that was lost and the best corals that were on the natural reef near Palm Jebel Ali were moved, along with two other major coral translocations, before they could be impacted. According to Nakheel, these translocated corals are thriving and have seeded the surrounding areas. While some marine biologists agree that the man-made reefs have not yet surpassed the natural reefs for coral diversity, they have also concluded that the average coral coverage on areas of man-made reefs has exceeded the natural reef.

However, marine experts at Abu Dhabi's Environment Agency worry that these artificial reefs aren't a true substitute for the areas that have been destroyed. By changing the marine environment, it's also possible that they may be affecting ecosystem balance leading to unforeseen impacts such as the loss of certain species or the flourishing of a certain predator at the expense of another species.

Dive centres do operate regular trips to sites at Palm Jumeirah and The World, so divers can go and judge for themselves.

DIVE 8

JASIM

Mottled ray

GPS
N24°58'47.2"
E54°29'43.8"

Depth: 27m | **Snorkelling:** No | **Night dive:** Yes
Distance from harbours:
Abu Dhabi Club 28.7nm @ 012°
DIMC 36nm @ 258°
Dubai Creek 46.9nm @ 246°
Jebel Ali Marina 28.9nm @ 268°

It's easy to become completely engrossed in this interesting dive, so keep an eye on your bottom time.

Once used by the UAE armed forces for target practice, the Jasim now rests on her port side, in 26-27m of water. She's broken into three large sections. The stern section consists of the engine room and accommodation, with the large single propeller and rudder still in place. The middle cargo section is a tangled, confused collection of broken hatches, rigging, old vehicle parts and lorry wheels. And the bow section still remains more or less intact with lamp rooms and deck winches.

Diving

This site is always an interesting dive, although care must be taken as the average depth is 27m. Watch your bottom time and allow plenty of air for safety stops. The bridge and living quarters can be accessed through several hatches. The engine room is a little more difficult to enter, although access can be gained through two deck hatches aft of the accommodation area. Once inside, take care not to stir up the deep layer of silt in the engine room.

THE FOG

A foggy mask can really ruin a dive or snorkel trip. Most people have tried any number of things in diving lore, but we have two favourite tricks.

The first is to rub a little toothpaste over the lens. This will get the fine layer of film off the mask (without damaging it) and it smells pretty good too. It's also a good idea to leave a little water in the mask until you put it on as this gets the mask to the same temperature as the sea.

If that doesn't do the job, try a squeeze of Johnson's Baby Shampoo in your mask and then rinse it just before you get into the water. And if you're not too thorough in cleaning the mask off, the beauty of it is... no more tears!

Marine Life

This wreck offers the opportunity to see the usual west coast marine life, including several species of brittle stars and cowrie shells. The shells are normally nocturnal, but on this site you can usually find one or two during the day.

There are also many hydrocorals, orange sponges and sea squirts. Although this wreck was sunk 20 years ago, the marine growth is not as advanced as it is on some of the west coast's other wrecks.

Wreck register: 108301272
Name: Jasim
Nationality: Unknown
Year built: Unknown
Type: MV coastal tanker
Tonnage: 1,200 tonnes gross
Dimensions: L: 60m, B: 10m, D: 5m
Cargo: Ballast
Date sunk: 25 March, 1986

Dottyback blenny

DIVE 9

JAZIRAT SIR BU NA'AIR

GPS
N25°13'30"
E54°13'00"

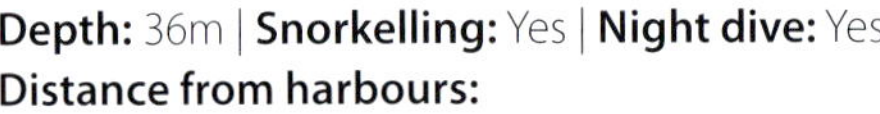

Depth: 36m | **Snorkelling:** Yes | **Night dive:** Yes

Distance from harbours:

Abu Dhabi Club 43.5nm @ 348°

DIMC 51.1nm @ 278°

Dubai Creek 58.7nm @ 266°

Jebel Ali Marina 46.3nm @ 286°

An island sanctuary for magnificent corals, turtles, rays and large pelagic fish.

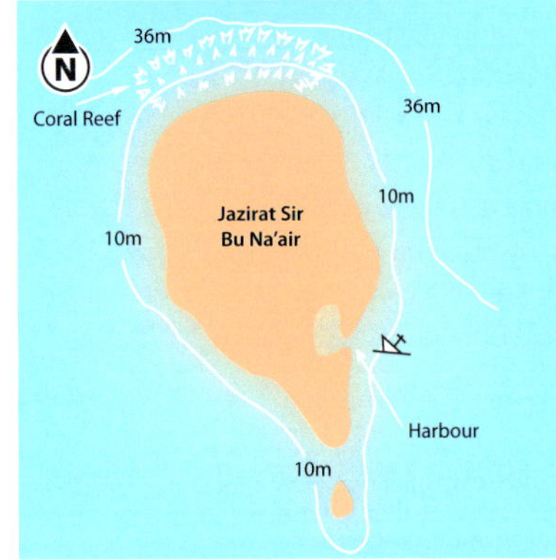

Jazirat Sir Bu Na'air is an island that lies 70km off the UAE coast. Measuring just over 1km long by 0.5km wide, it's a UAE military outpost and coastguard station, but also a protected turtle breeding area. There are no restrictions on sailing or diving near the island, but it is a sensitive military base so landing is not advisable (although you do occasionally see people picnicking on the beaches).

In 2000, HH Dr Sheikh Sultan bin Mohammed Al Qassimi, Supreme Council Member and Ruler of Sharjah, issued Administrative Order No. 3 that banned all activities considered harmful to the environment of Jazirat Sir Bu Na'air island. The six article order seeks to halt the deterioration of the island's environment, protect its marine life, and develop its natural resources. This means that fishing all species of turtle, collecting their eggs or damaging their nesting beaches along the island's coastline is strictly prohibited.

The order also bans any activities that could threaten the safety of the island's many resident and migrating bird species.

Diving

This site is characterised by coral reefs, a shelving sandy bottom and lots of drop-offs. Towards the northern end of the island there's a large area of table and staghorn coral in magnificent condition. The coral runs north to the 20m mark and then the seabed shelves down to a depth of more than 30m.

The north-eastern side has large flat rocks and coral, and there are more extensive areas of coral to the north-west. Off the southern tip of the island, the sandy bottom runs to 20m, ending with a small sea mount. At the entrance to the harbour on the south-east side, you'll find the partially submerged wreck of a barge.

Snorkelling

The island isn't just for divers – snorkellers will have a wonderful time here too. The visibility is good, and as it is one of the protected turtle breeding areas, turtles are frequently seen by snorkellers. By using a snorkel, you create less noise and fewer bubbles than divers do, so it's easier to get a closer look at the marine life.

Concentrate on the northern coral field, which starts at 5m and runs gently into deeper water.

Green turtle

Marine Life

The island is rarely visited by divers or fishermen and the resulting lack of disturbance encourages prolific shoals of fish. There are numerous large pelagic fish, spotted eagle rays, barracuda and large rays.

It's a long journey to the island, but the diving and snorkelling at Jazirat Sir Bu Na'air is definitely worth the trip.

THE BIG QUEASY

There are a number of sea sickness tablets you can take – Dramamine, Stugeron and Dezinil – and you may have to try them all out (on different dives, of course) to determine which one suits you best. Some divers wear wristbands with special pressure points on the wrists, or patches that look like mini plasters. Called Scopoderm, they are worn behind the ears and can be quite effective. As with all medication, you need to take care of the possible side-effects.

There are also other ways to minimise the chance of feeling seasick. When you're getting ready for a dive try to have all your gear lined up and placed within easy reach. This will enable you to kit up quickly – the last thing you want is to be looking down for any length of time. While you're on the boat, try to keep your eyes on the horizon.

If you feel sick after surfacing, you'll feel better if you remove your gear and get back into the water (if it's not rough). Also, make sure you drink plenty of fluids to avoid becoming dehydrated.

DIVE 10

LION CITY

Shoals of snapper

GPS
N25°00'13.4"
E54°31'43.9"

Depth: 30m | **Snorkelling:** No | **Night dive:** Yes
Distance from harbours:
Abu Dhabi Club 30.4nm @ 014°
DIMC 33.9nm @ 259°
DOSC 38.8nm @ 253°
Jebel Ali Marina 27nm @ 270°

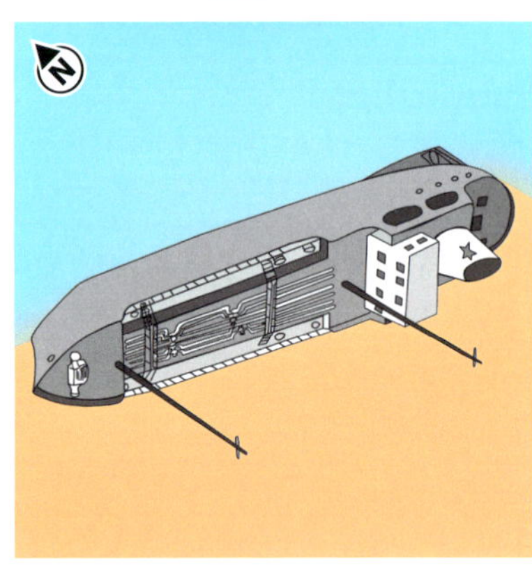

An exercise in orientation and navigation that makes a good second dive.

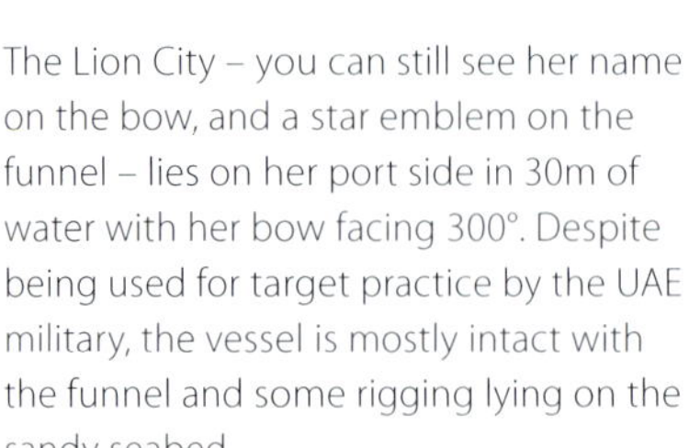

The Lion City – you can still see her name on the bow, and a star emblem on the funnel – lies on her port side in 30m of water with her bow facing 300°. Despite being used for target practice by the UAE military, the vessel is mostly intact with the funnel and some rigging lying on the sandy seabed.

The distance from the shore makes this wreck a good second dive if you've been exploring either the Jasim (see p.26) or the MV Ludwig (see p.38), which are not too far away.

Diving

The Lion City's living quarters and engine rooms are easily accessed without much difficulty. If you do want to enter and investigate the interior, remember that the wreck is lying on its side, so keep this in mind when navigating your way around. Swimming along stairways that don't go up or down and arriving in rooms on their side can be disorientating.

Look at the shape of holes in the wreck and decide which is the easiest way for you to fit through. Don't forget that with your tank and BCD you are now deeper than you are wide. If you feel yourself becoming stuck, reverse immediately – before you really do get stuck!

On the deck, the oil transfer pipes run almost from the bridge to the bosun's storerooms forward, covering most of the available deck space. This is an interesting area to search for unusual marine life.

Marine Life

The marine growth has been slower to colonise this wreck than it has on others, but it began with the formation of some white coral patches on the deck and on the upper side of the hull. Covering large areas of the hull, these corals grow in circular patches about 100mm across. Hydrocorals, looking like mini fir trees, have given the hull a dull light brown colour. On one of the walkways across the pipes, a colony of white soft corals has taken up residence on the treads and handrails.

Shoals of yellow coloured blackspot snapper swim over and under the labyrinth of pipes on the Jasim's deck hunting for their quarry. These little hunters are distinctively coloured and sport a black spot under the dorsal fins and longitudinal yellow pinstripes. They work equally well in packs, or on their own when they wait in the shadows for their dinner to come to them.

Wreck register: 108300171
Name: Lion City
Nationality: Unknown
Year built: Unknown
Type: MV Coastal tanker
Tonnage: 1,200 tonnes gross
Dimensions: L: 60m, B: 10m, D: 5m
Cargo: Ballast
Date sunk: 1 May, 1986

HEAVY METAL

The high temperatures, humidity and salinity of the Gulf means that your dive gear will take a bit more strain than in other parts of the world. It's essential that you have your cylinders visually inspected once a year, and hydro-tested every five years here.

Aeolid nudibranch

DIVE 11

MARIAM EXPRESS

Depth: 21m | **Snorkelling:** No | **Night dive:** No
Distance from harbours:
DIMC 21.8nm @ 355°
Dubai Creek 14.7nm @ 316°

One of the newer wrecks, she is home to unusual cargo and varied marine life.

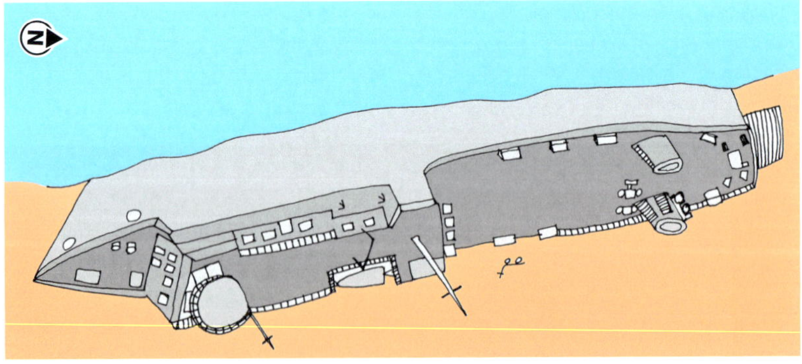

Lloyds Casualty Register notes that the Mariam Express was overloaded when she encountered strong winds and moderate seas en-route to Iraq. She took on water and sunk rapidly. All crew were rescued.

Diving

The Mariam Express lies on her port side with the bow facing 150°. Visibility on the site is usually remarkably good, averaging 10m, but as she gets older and more silt gathers, it could reduce.

A buoy marks the aft section of the wreck. It's recommended that you go down the anchor and make your way to the bow. Inspect the bow area, then ascend a little to explore the hold. In one hold you'll find a number of tea sets all neatly packed in polystyrene, numerous bundles of quilt bedding, and piles of electrical games scattered about. There are even a couple of JCBs in one of the holds, along with twin tub washing machines and numerous scooters (one of which lies outside the hold).

When you're descending the anchor chain, you'll notice orange pieces of debris swaying in the current: this is the aft life raft which has been broken into three pieces, two of which are hanging on precariously. There's also plenty of debris on the seabed to pick over: rope ladders, tyres, broken crockery and so on. Don't forget to allow yourself time to inspect the masts and the deck railings. As the top of the wreck is at 8m, make the most of the dive and enjoy a last lingering look around while completing your safety stop.

Although a night dive on the Mariam would be possible, it's not recommended while there is any construction work in the area.

Marine Life

After only a few months of submersion, the Mariam Express wreck boasted a variety of fish life, which increases with time. Large barracuda hang out at the bow, enjoying the currents, while juvenile barracuda hide in the hold with the crockery and bedding.

The wreck is smothered with small oyster shells, and between the gaps you'll find numerous colonial ascidians or sea squirts in different colours – white, yellow, green, red or orange – as well as small anemones. The wreck also hosts the usual snappers, pennantfish and jacks. You may find a pair of resident sabretooth blennies, but their camouflage is excellent, making them difficult to spot

Oysters

WARNING

As with any wreck, take care as you may cut or hurt yourself on jagged edges or protrusions. You should only try to penetrate the vessel if you're trained in wreck diving.

Crested sabretooth blenny

Wreck register: Not charted
Name: Delos Express
Nationality: Panamanian, re-registered in France
Year built: 1978
Type: Roll-on roll-off vessel
Tonnage: 3,348 tonnes gross
Dimensions: L: 94m, B: 13m, D: 8m
Cargo: Household and electrical goods, scooters
Date sunk: 2 May, 2006

DIVE 12

MV DARA

GPS

N25°34'29.0"
E55°27'58.6"

Depth: 18m | **Snorkelling:** No | **Night dive:** Yes

Distance from harbours:

DOSC 27.4nm @ 028°
Dubai Creek 20.3nm @ 025°
Hamriya Harbour 5.8nm @ 347°
Sharjah Creek 12.5nm @ 019°

The disastrous sinking of the MV Dara has resulted in a difficult, but rewarding wreck dive.

The MV Dara was a passenger liner built in 1948 by Barclay Curle & Co. of Glasgow, UK. Fitted with a single Doxford oil engine, she was operated by the British India Steam Navigation Company.

The story of the disaster is well documented. The following information has been compiled from *Last Hours on the Dara* by PJ Abraham, *The Grey-Widow Maker* by Bernard Edward and an article by Ian Bain that first appeared in the *Khaleej Times Magazine* on 4 April, 1980.

The Dara sailed between Bombay, Karachi, the Gulf and the ports of Basra, Kuwait, Bahrain, Dubai and Muscat, carrying passengers, mail and cargo. During the early hours of 8 April, 1961, after putting to sea on 7 April to weather out a storm, a bomb planted on her by an Omani rebel exploded. It's believed that the bomb was timed to explode when the Dara berthed at Muscat, but due to the storm, her departure from Dubai had been delayed. The bomb was planted to further the cause of the Dhofar rebellion; the uprising against Sultan Said bin Taimur, the

rather erratic and isolated ruler of Oman, who was finally replaced in a bloodless coup by his son, the present Sultan.

The explosion between decks started a fire that raged for two days and caused considerable loss of life. The fire was finally extinguished, but the ship sank while under tow by Ocean Salvor, a salvage vessel. The final figure was 238 deaths; the second greatest number of fatalities recorded at sea in peacetime after the Titanic disaster.

The MV Dara is now owned by Clive Frost of Aqua Diving Services.

Diving

The Dara lies on her starboard side at 18m, broken into three sections. Every season the superstructure collapses further, limiting access to the wreck, although it is still possible to enter through the stern.

This site can be quite dangerous as the tides can be very strong and visibility poor as a result. On a neap tide, though, this is an excellent dive. Just be aware of abandoned fishing nets, and dive with a knife in case you become entangled.

Marine Life

One of the unique species of marine life that you're likely to see on this site are the cowries of the cypraea histro and arabica varieties. Their shells have absorbed the iron oxide from the rusting wreck, giving them a metallic reddish-brown colour.

The Dara also attracts many species of rays; shovelnose guitarfish, eagle rays and even feather tailed stingrays. The site is usually covered with snapper and, in the cooler months, barracuda, and it's occasionally visited by whale sharks.

Wreck register: 108300171
Name: MV Dara
Nationality: British
Year built: 1948
Type: Passenger liner
Tonnage: 5.030 tonnes
Dimensions: L: 121m, B: 17m, D: 15m
Cargo: Mail and cargo
Date sunk: 10 April, 1961

DIVE 13

MV HANNAN

Warty Doris nudibranch

GPS
N24°50'11.0"
E53°53'34.0"

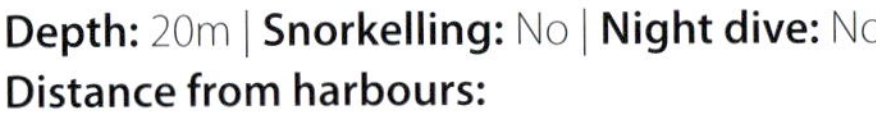

Depth: 20m | **Snorkelling:** No | **Night dive:** No
Distance from harbours:
Abu Dhabi Club 33nm @ 306°
Jebel Ali Marina 62.5nm @ 260°

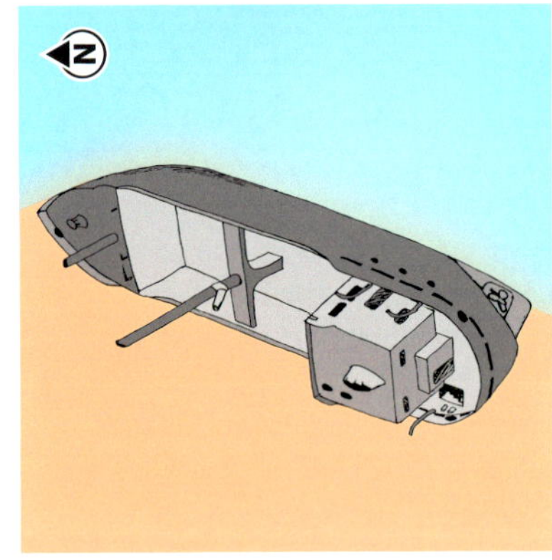

Practise your wreck penetration skills and hunt for warty Doris and other residents.

Given her position near the offshore rigs and platforms, it's logical to conclude that the MV Hannan sank while working in the Abu Dhabi oil fields.

Diving

The Hannan is a small coastal vessel that lies with her stern roughly pointing towards the north. Two buoys mark the site; the official cardinal wreck buoy, and a huge barrel with a large chain link that's anchored less than 3m from the stern on the starboard side.

Once you've descended, start from the seabed and go around the wreck in a clockwise direction towards the bow. You'll need to ascend a little in order to explore the hold area that's split in two by a small derrick. You can try some wreck penetration; you might be able to access the bridge and accommodation areas via a small window or via the companionway door. If you go through the door and out of the small window at the top of the wheelhouse, you'll find a small object that looks like a left-over treasure box.

Ascidians, also called sea squirts

Marine Life

As a result of the currents, you'll find large shoals of fish congregating on this wreck, including various species of jacks such as yellow striped jacks and finger jacks (also known as queenfish). The shoals share the currents with large, mean looking barracuda, some of which have unusual barred markings. The site is also home to some very big hammour that measure more than a metre in length, as well as large pufferfish and batfish.

Among the rays you'll see are bell, leopard, eagle and electric rays and guitar sharks. The rays are sometimes seen on the upper surfaces of the hull and companionways, looking for the nudibranchs that cling to the surfaces. If you join them, you may find one of the largest nudibranchs in the Gulf. Nicknamed 'warty Doris', these creatures grow to about 125mm. Although it's large, (by nudibranch standards) warty Doris is also well camouflaged and easily overlooked.

The site also has some inhabitants not seen regularly in the Gulf. There are small translucent colonial ascidians (delicate sea squirts) and an unusual purple soft coral that's formed in clumps all over the wreck.

Safety

The currents on this site can be very strong and, as it's located well offshore, assistance may not be immediately available. You should also carry a dive knife or net cutters as this site is liberally covered with old nets.

COOL CRITTERS

Some of the most colourful members of the marine world are the nudibranchs. The name translates into 'naked gill', and they either have their gills prominently displayed on their backs, or in a tuft at the posterior end.

As they're basically naked snails, nudibranchs have developed alternative defence systems. They're usually vividly coloured to try to persuade other sea life that they won't make a good main course. Many secrete a strong scent and others feed on sea anemones and hydroids – and use their lunch's stinging cells as their own defence mechanism.

Nudibranchs make excellent photographic subjects if you're into underwater micro photography – they're brilliantly coloured and not inclined to move very fast.

Wreck register: Not charted
Name: MV Hannan
Nationality: Unknown
Year built: Unknown
Type: Coastal vessel single screw oil engine
Tonnage: 288 tonnes gross
Dimensions: L: 42m, B: 6.5m, D: 2.6m
Cargo: None
Date sunk: 3 August, 1986

DIVE 14

MV LUDWIG

GPS
N25°06'53.8"
E54°34'14.1"

Depth: 27m | **Snorkelling:** No | **Night dive:** Yes
Distance from harbours:
Abu Dhabi Club 37.3nm @ 015°
DIMC 31.2nm @ 271°
DOSC 35.3nm @ 262°
Jebel Ali Marina 26nm @ 286°

Once used as target practice, this wreck is now host to a growing marine community.

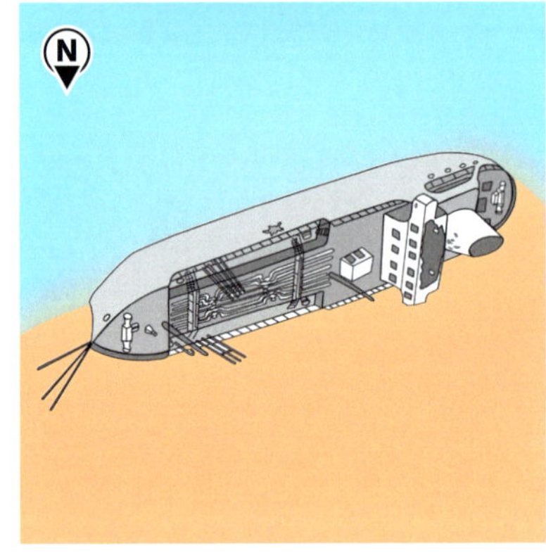

The large 1,200 tonne MV Ludwig is more or less intact and lies on her port side, with her bow pointing east at 70°, in 27m of water.

The UAE armed forces used the Ludwig for target practice and they were very accurate! The bridge received a direct hit and the explosion ripped out the internal walls and roof of the bridge. Damage can also be seen on the funnel, where shrapnel from the bridge punched holes in it. There is another projectile exit hole on the starboard side of the hull.

Diving

You can begin your exploration of the inside of the wreck via the bridge section, working your way down into the crew quarters or going through the stern hatches into the engine room.

The wreck is very similar to the Lion City (p.30), as the deck on both is a maze of oil transfer pipes and valves. You could almost be fooled into thinking you were diving the Lion City, as both ships were coastal oil tankers and both lie on their port sides. However, the MV Ludwig is larger and has two bridges over the pipe runs, as well as a small deckhouse forward of the bridge.

Marine Life

The marine growth on the Ludwig is developing well; hydrocorals and sea squirts were among the first inhabitants. The wreck's pipes and rigging offer security to a profusion of reef fish, such as the shoals of pennantfish that glide over structures in close formation and the damselfish that dart in and out of the cover of the iron and steel.

A large resident shoal of yellow snappers seeks security inside the wreck from the hordes of barracuda that constantly circle outside, while batfish live further out.

Shoals of yellow snapper

Bannerfish

SMELLY WETSUIT CURES

Many divers have a warm-up trick that they'd rather keep quiet about. The evidence, however, lies in how their wetsuit smells . . .

Warming your suit 'the natural way' does provide a thermal boost, but it also allows bacteria to set up home in your wetsuit, and not even a good rinse can get rid of that.

There are a few products on the market that do help: the main one is called Sink The Stink, and it consists of a small capsule of deodorising liquid that's very effective at killing the bacteria and making your suit smell sweet (well, of neoprene) once again.

Wreck register: Not charted
Name: MV Ludwig
Nationality: Unknown
Year built: Unknown
Type: MV coastal tanker
Tonnage: 1,200 tonnes gross
Dimensions: L: 60m, B: 10m, D: 5m
Cargo: Ballast
Year sunk: 2000

DIVE 15

NASTERAN

GPS
N25°28'00.0"
E55°21'22.0"

Depth: 23m | **Snorkelling:** No | **Night dive:** Yes
Distance from harbours:
DIMC 25.2nm @ 028°
Dubai Creek 12nm @ 0.15°
Hamriya Harbour 7.4nm @ 262°
Sharjah Creek 5.6nm @ 341°

This site offers a good opportunity to practise your wreck diving skills... and to search for sea hares.

The Nasteran lies completely upside down in 23m of water, with her bow or landing door facing the shore at 150°. The wheelhouse lies to the east, next to the starboard side of the vessel, and both her propellers have been cut off.

Diving

Access to the accommodation and engine room is through a hole near the wheelhouse on the east side of the wreck, but note that this route is very silted.

The deck area forward of the wheelhouse is also worth a visit, but you'll need a torch to illuminate the fish life and marine growth.

Entry into the cargo area is through the partially open landing doors. If you're lucky, you could find some surprises in here, such as the blind juvenile sharks that like to hide away in the darker areas of the vessel.

There's a lot of silt throughout the wreck, so pay attention to your finning techniques as you could easily reduce the visibility to zero. And if you're planning on penetrating the Nasteran, it's advisable that you use a line and torch at all times.

Marine Life

If you take the time to explore the upturned hull you're likely to be rewarded with the sight of many of the smaller creatures that are often overlooked; look out for shells, shrimps, nudibranchs, small blennies and unusual creatures called sea hares.

Sea hares are members of the shell family and are called 'hares' because of their rabbit-like appearance. They have two rolled rhinophores (sensory organs) on their head that seem to give them rabbits' ears, and two flaps, known as parapodia, to aid swimming. They are herbivorous and feed on algae and sea grasses – which means that the Nasteran's hull is a regular smorgasbord for them.

Wreck register: 108300201
Name: Nasteran
Nationality: Iranian registered
Year built: Unknown
Type: Landing craft
Tonnage: 652 tonnes gross
Dimensions: L: 62m, B: 10m, D: 8m
Cargo: Stones
Date sunk: 14 March, 1970

Sea hare

Two strombus shells courting

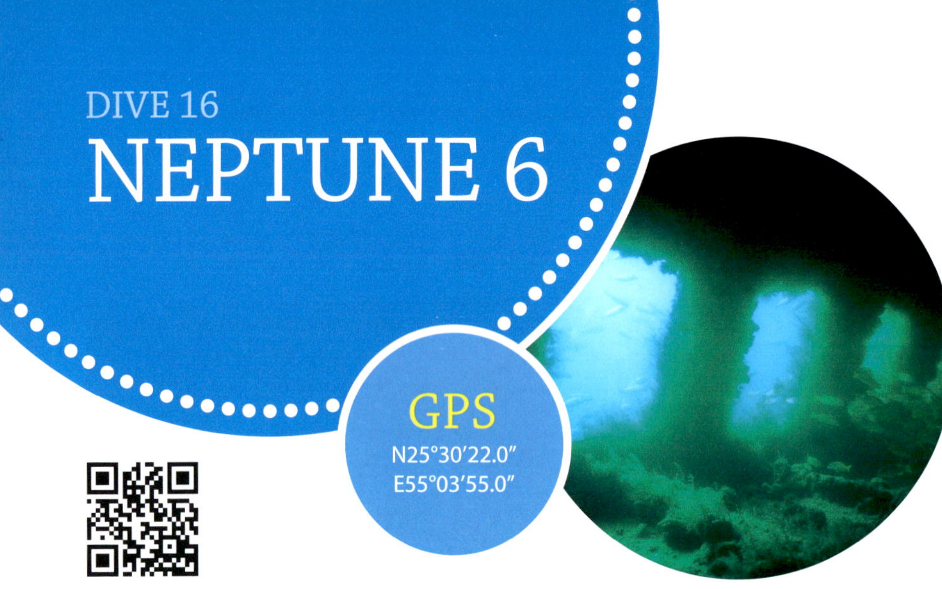

DIVE 16

NEPTUNE 6

GPS
N25°30'22.0"
E55°03'55.0"

Depth: 23m | **Snorkelling:** No | **Night dive:** Yes
Distance from harbours:
DIMC 25nm @ 349°
DOSC 21.5nm @ 022°
Dubai Creek 18.7nm @ 317°
Distance to other dive sites:
To Hopper Barge 6 (p.20) 0.18nm @ 043°
To Anchor Barge (p.6) 0.7nm @ 055°

It's a long way offshore, but this is an excellent dive with the promise of 'treasure' to be found.

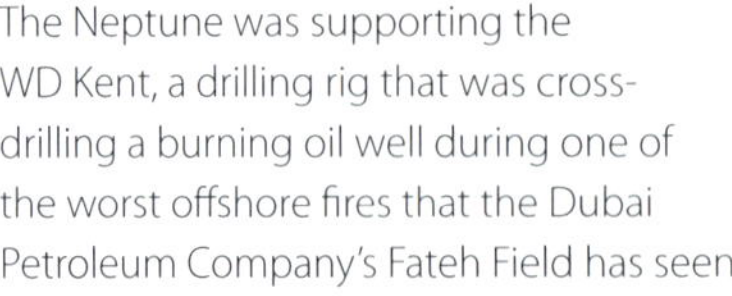

The Neptune was supporting the WD Kent, a drilling rig that was cross-drilling a burning oil well during one of the worst offshore fires that the Dubai Petroleum Company's Fateh Field has seen.

The Neptune pulled off during bad weather, but dragged her anchor and ended up colliding with the WD Kent, ultimately sinking the rig. After the collision, it was decided that the Neptune would be taken to Sharjah. However, she capsized while under tow and sank in her present position.

Diving

The vessel lies upside down in 25m of water with her bow facing 151°. There's a considerable amount of debris, including a crane boom, drilling equipment and wreckage from the deck accommodation, along her port side. There can be strong currents at this site, making exploration quite difficult. For many years, the main entrance into the wreck was on the starboard side, a third of the way along the hull from the stern. Now that the wreck is breaking up though, access is possible on both the port and starboard sides, and you can swim all the way through.

Although this site is 18.7nm from shore, it's usually an excellent dive. There are also three other wrecks within a 1nm radius of the Neptune; the Anchor Barge (p.6, Hopper Barge 6 (p.20) and the Morafi Barge (the Morafi is of little interest though, and rarely dived).

Marine Life

The fish life tends to congregate on the Neptune's port side, although you often find stingrays if you swim out beyond the wreckage.

The crane structure is home to a colony of white soft coral, that is very beautiful when illuminated.

Octocoral

After circling the wreck, examine its surface where you'll find shrimps, blennies and octocorals (so called because they have eight feather-like tentacles or pinnates). The octocorals are tiny and come in many colours. They can live as individuals or in colonies. Some are purely soft and feathery; some have an internal skeleton composed of a type of calcareous material; and others still use another subject as a base from which to sprout. Take the time to watch their polyps pulse as they feed. The coral colonies pulsate at different speeds and the effect is quite hypnotic!

Wreck register: 108300055
Name: Neptune 6
Nationality: Panamanian registered
Year built: Unknown
Type: Drill rig tender barge
Tonnage: 2,300 tonnes gross
Dimensions: L: 79m, B: 15m, D: 8m
Cargo: General drilling equipment
Date sunk: 12 November, 1973

UP CLOSE AND PERSONAL

Honeycomb moray

Tobyfish

Turtle

Frogfish

Arabian stonefish

DIVE 17

SWIFT

GPS

N25° 27'37.7"
E54° 17'41.2"

Depth: 38m | **Snorkelling:** No | **Night dive:** No
Distance from harbours:
DIMC 51.1nm @ 294°
Dubai Creek 55.4nm @ 280°
DOSC 52.8nm @ 288°

A deep and seldom-dived wreck with good marine life and the odd treasure still to be seen.

Swift sank following a collision with the Brown and Root pipe-laying barge No. 207, while working in the SW Fateh Oil Field. Today the vessel sits upright and intact on the sand, and stands 15m high in 38m of water. Her location is close to the Dubai Petroleum Company (DPC) and Dubai Natural Gas Company's SW Fateh oil and gas platforms.

Diving

This site is a long way offshore and is only occasionally dived, which is probably the reason why the fish seem almost tame. The wreck is located just 2.5nm (4.6km) away from the oil and gas platforms, so take care to keep to the south west of the oil field. DPC have strict procedures regarding access to the area. Unauthorised boats will be visited by the coast guard.

The water clarity is usually good this far out, and you can expect the visibility to be between 15 and 20m. When you descend, the first thing you're likely to see is the white soft corals that cover most of the wreck and give it an eerie glow.

There are several ways into the wreck for adventurous divers who are trained in wreck penetration. At times the wreck can be found draped in fishing nets, making access and exploration difficult. Ensure that you carry a small knife with you so that you're able to cut the nets if you get snagged in them.

Marine Life

The white soft telesto corals (octocorals) are spectacular; they look like a blanket of snow that covers large sections of the vessel. Shoals of yellow and black striped jacks and snappers circle the wreck, parting and regrouping as you swim through them.

The marine life is well established and every surface is covered in layers of barnacles, oyster shells and hard and soft corals all competing for space. There are many holes and crevices for little creatures to dart in and out of, making this a very interesting dive.

Blubberlip snapper

WHICH ONE'S MINE, AGAIN?

Ever been on a busy dive boat and unable to find your gear because everyone's looks the same? A few minutes spent writing your name and mobile number on your equipment with a special marker pen will see you getting into the water first from now on.

And if you leave something behind or someone picks it up by mistake, you may even be lucky enough to get a phone call to set up a happy reunion.

Wreck register: 108202021 (wreck no. 43707)
Name: Claudine, renamed Swift
Nationality: Bahraini
Year built: Unknown
Type: Motor tug
Tonnage: Unknown
Dimensions: L: 27.4m, B: 7.3m, D: 3.7m
Cargo: Unknown
Date sunk: 21 February, 1987

DIVE 18

TURTLE BARGE

GPS

N25°26’43.2”
E55°26’57.6”

Depth: 8m | **Snorkelling:** Yes | **Night dive:** Yes

Distance from harbours:

Hamriya Harbour 3.1 nm. @ 226°
Sharjah Creek 5.2 nm. @ 39°

An easy-to-access site that’s home to fascinating corals, along with a friendly turtle.

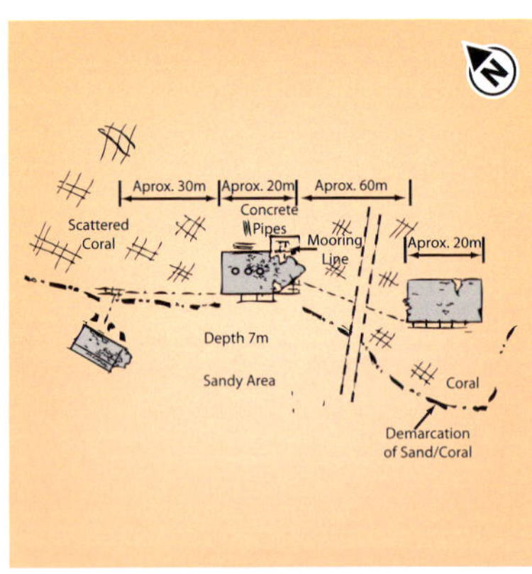

This is probably a small barge that’s been scattered over a large area in three parts or large pieces of wreckage, but it could even be two small wrecks. The site was discovered by Blue Planet Diving in 1999 when divers were training outside the harbour wall in Ajman. The circumstances around the loss of the wreck (or wrecks) aren’t known.

Diving

The wreckage lies just five minutes outside the Ajman harbour, so access is quick and easy and the site is excellent for night diving. As it’s rather shallow it’s also a good wreck site for snorkellers to explore.

The wreck is fairly flat but full of holes that provide an ideal home for all kinds of marine life. A length of rope stretches about 60m between the two main pieces of wreckage to make navigation easier. There are some large pipes alongside one of the main pieces of wreckage and various bits and pieces littered about. It’s easy to become disorientated due to the various pieces of debris, but as it’s a nice shallow site you can simply surface and wait for the dive boat to collect you.

When diving here, please use the mooring buoy that Blue Planet Diving has created out of numerous bottles. This means you don't have to throw the anchor in and damage the corals.

Marine Life

As you descend the mooring buoy you'll be greeted by a lone clownfish who has made his home under the mooring line. And as the name suggests, you're also likely to encounter the friendly turtle that has taken up residence on the wreckage.

This is an attractive site with an incredibly large number of hard corals spread over the seabed and wreckage. There are colonies of different coral families growing on top of one another, competing for space and light. If you look closely, you'll see the corals are almost fluorescent, and glow with hues of orange, green, red and blue.

The west coast regulars are all here: yellow snappers, blennies, monos, hammour and barracuda. On closer inspection, you may also see nudibranchs, various types of sponges and shells – especially if you bring a torch.

This is an ideal site for students, but even well-dived instructors will find something to enjoy on this dive. If you're particularly keen to see many varieties of hard coral in a small area, this is a must.

Wreck register: Not charted
Name: Unknown
Nationality: Unknown
Year built: Unknown
Type: MV coastal barge – single screw
Tonnage: Unknown
Dimensions: Unknown
Cargo: None
Date sunk: Unknown

WARNING

Take care not to get your equipment or yourself caught on the wreckage and always wear protective clothing.

Green turtle

DIVE 19

VICTORIA STAR

GPS
N25°24'8.30"
E 55°16'11.70"

Depth: 22m | **Snorkelling:** No | **Night dive:** Yes
Distance from harbours:
DIMC 18.68nm @ 028°
DOSC 13.23nm @ 019°

As a new wreck she only has a few fish, but the site is improving very quickly, and is suitable for most levels.

The Victoria Star sank around August or September 2013 after being hit by another vessel. She sits almost perfectly upright in 22m of water but is in an area many vessels use to approach the harbour and so has no cardinal buoy. She was carrying a small cargo of insulated concrete blocks when she sank, and they are now scattered in the two main holds. The top of the bridge is around 12m and the deck around 16m. Dropping into the holds will take you past the 18m mark, but there is plenty to keep your attention around the bridge area.

Diving

There is very little on the bottom so start by swimming around at deck level on one side and then back on the other side. Drop down into the holds and check out the cargo. Most of the fish life will also be here waiting for you. Once you get to the stern, drop down to the propeller and then back up. The bridge area covers two levels with plenty still intact to explore. Initially, when the ship sank, the life rafts were still attached to their anchor points but unfortunately are no longer there.

Both external doors to the bridge have

Arabian angelfish

been removed and make for an easy swim through. There is also a narrow corridor leading to a lower deck for tech divers and those who are a little more adventurous. Plus, there are numerous doors leading to different rooms on the first level. Be careful as many of the doors and contents have yet to be removed. There are also doors leading to small storerooms on the deck level but, again, doors and content have yet to be removed so watch your fingers. There are numerous manholes on the stern and bow leading to lower areas. These are good areas for experienced wreck divers.

Victoria Star is always worth a visit. Given her location it's not often the best visibility, but that's what makes it an exciting and mysterious wreck to dive. The current can also arrive with little notice so be prepared just in case. On occasion, mainly when items are being removed, there is still the smell of diesel fuel lingering in the air at the surface. She is a good night dive but the distance to travel safely at night will add to your return travel time.

Marine Life

Given the Victoria Star has been underwater for only one year (at the time of writing), marine growth is good. There are areas of sponges, ascidians, sea squirts and barnacles from one end to the other. The fish life is mostly small schools of snapper, monocle bream and batfish found in the two holds; and the occasional hammour swimming around the bridge area. There are small crabs hiding throughout so look carefully, you never know what you'll find. The life living on this wreck is increasing all the time.

IMO register: 7111004
Name: Victoria Star
Nationality: Sierra Leone (SL)
Year built: 1972
Type: General cargo
Tonnage: Gross tonnage 1,485 kg
Dimensions: L: 80m, B: 12m, D: 10m
Cargo: Concrete blocks
Date sunk: Aug/Sept 2013

DIVE 20

ZAINAB

GPS
N25°14'55.8"
E54°51'32.4"

Depth: 29m | **Snorkelling:** No | **Night dive:** Yes
Distance from harbours:
DIMC 18.1nm @ 300°
DOSC 20nm @ 281°
Dubai Creek 23.8nm @ 265°

An interesting dive not only for Zainab's illicit past, but also for her present day marine life.

The Zainab, formerly called the Seasroun Five, sailed under a Georgian flag and was involved in the illegal transportation of light fuel oil from Iraq when she went down.

She was a general cargo ship with two holds forward and the machinery, bridge and quarters aft. To conceal her illegal cargo, her holds had been converted to hold the oil. She was carrying about 1,300 tonnes of fuel oil when she was deliberately sunk by her 11 man crew to avoid being boarded by the US Navy, who were enforcing UN sanctions on Iraq. The sinking resulted in a major oil spill on the northern Gulf coast, and caused serious concern to the local gas processing plant as she sank within a few hundred metres of their offshore gas pipelines. The story was documented by *Gulf News* throughout April 2001.

Diving

The Zainab is intact and lies on her port side, with the anchor still sitting snug on the bow. The covers of the holds are off and lie on the sea bed at about 29m. There are various bits and pieces of debris and artefacts strewn over the seabed; you'll find an empty compass binnacle, an upside down life raft at the stern and an industrial fire extinguisher on the seabed below the propeller.

The bridge, and the engine and accommodation rooms are easily accessible. But be sure that you can see daylight at the other end, before you enter the vessel.

This is one of the deeper dive sites on this coast and, at over 70m long, it's a fairly large wreck. You should be able to explore it in one dive though. A suggested dive plan is to start at the most interesting area, which is the now vertical deck. Make your way along the wreck and past the open hatches; their doors lie haphazardly on the seabed, looking like a discarded pack of cards. Investigate the upturned life raft when you reach the stern and, if you have enough time, take a look at the fire extinguisher that lies just beneath the propeller. Ascend slowly, exploring the bridge and decks aft. The remaining life raft is swinging from one davit. Go around the wreck and look at the propeller. Then return to the top of the wreck, at approximately 20m.

Wreck register: Not charted
Name: Zainab, originally known as The Seasroun Five
Nationality: Georgian registered
Year built: Unknown
Type: General cargo ship
Tonnage: 1,400 tonnes gross
Dimensions: L: 70m, B: 12m, D: 5m
Cargo: Fuel oil
Date sunk: 14 April, 2001

Fire fighting equipment

A night dive on the Zainab is possible for more experienced divers, but it's a long way offshore.

Marine Life

During the time the Zainab has been down, it has attracted a large variety of marine life. The wreck is carpeted with small oysters, and juvenile fish weave their way in and out of their shell homes. Most avoid contact with divers, but some are very inquisitive and allow you to get close to them.

You may find large rays resting on the seabed, and huge shoals of barracuda circling the wreck. You will often find large shoals of yellow snappers swimming round the various masts towards the bow, and there's usually a shoal of batfish that congregates near the bridge and wheelhouse.

ABU DHABI DIVES

Seahorse

There are many sites to dive in Abu Dhabi's waters. Here are our favourite new discoveries...

DIVE 21
AL DHABIYAH CORAL GARDEN

GPS
N24°23'60.00"
E54° 4'48.00"

Depth: 10m

Coral

Al Dhabiyah Coral Garden is located approximately 30km west of Abu Dhabi. It has a sandy bottom with a variety of hard corals and is a beautiful scenic dive. Usually there are shoals of yellow snappers, along with goatfish, a curious family of batfish that follow the divers, hammour, yellow bar angel fish, bennies, sandy gobies and commensal shrimps. If you look closely you can also find some anemones with clown fish living in them.

There are plenty of juvenile fish around and, when the water temperature is around 25°C, there will be rays on the seabed, including stingrays, leopard rays, butterfly rays, torpedo rays, feather tail rays and shovelnose rays. Some divers have also seen bamboo sharks. Also, look for seahorses in the seagrass area.

Take special care to avoid damaging the hard corals and practise good buoyancy control whilst keeping fin tips up rather than downwards. Sometimes there can be a moderate current, and so all divers should carry a Delayed Surface Marker Buoy (DSMB) so you can be easily located by the dive boat.

Al Mahara Diving Center regularly dives this site. It is also the selected site for the Reef Check Coral monitoring programme run by Emirates Diving Association (EDA) and Al Mahara.

DIVE 22
CAR CEMETERY

GPS
N24°16'48.00"
E52°39'36.00"

Depth: 14-16m

Car Cemetery is located east of Sir Bani Yas Island, only a few kilometres from the coast. There are 20-25 cars lying together in a large sandy sloping area. Look out for batfish, giant hammour, barracuda, trevallies, snappers and the Arabian angel fish, which are abundant. Blennies and dottybacks are usually hiding in crevices. Stingrays and hawksbill and green sea turtles have also been spotted on this site. As the site is close to Stewart Channel, it is important to carry a DSMB and keep a visual of the car wrecks. Nearby is the Pearl wreck.

DIVE 23

GASHA BUOY RIG

GPS
N24°28'48.00"
E53° 6'36.00"

Depth: 14-19m

This rig is about 30km from the mainland, and 4.1nm north of Sir Bani Yas Island. Only a few divers have ventured here due to its isolated location. Permission must be obtained by Ruwais Petroleum Port Authority before visiting. Desert Islands Watersports Center can arrange diving trips in this area.

You can see schools of snappers, jacks, queenfish, angelfish, hawksbill turtles, stingrays, soft corals, nudibranchs, and a large school of batfish.

Sometimes moderate current and low visibility can make it hard to find. Also, be careful of abandoned fishing lines. Always make a safety stop and deploy a Surface Marker Buoy (SMB).

Nudibranch

DIVE 24

HOOK ISLAND

GPS
N24°21'44.14"
E52°45'46.10"

Depth: 15m

Hook Island is approximately 11km east of Sir Bani Yas Island. The dive follows a slope on the inside of a crater-shaped island.

Boats should anchor north east of the slope taking care not to come in too shallow, and divers then swim to the site.

You'll see various species of hard coral including porites, acropora and favia. There are plenty of snappers, angelfish, giant hammour, two-striped breams, trevallies, butterfly fish, and also stingrays and green sea turtles have also been spotted on this site.

To arrive at the site from Sir Bani Yas Island you must cross the Stewart Channel; therefore, permission must be obtained by Ruwais Petroleum Port Authority.

Aeolid nudibranch

DIVE 25
PEARL WRECK

GPS
N24°16'48.00"
E52°39'36.00"

Depth: 12m

The Pearl is a small supply vessel, east of Sir Bani Yas Island, a few kilometres from the island's coast. She's sitting upright, and is about 30m in length. The roof is close enough to the surface that it's visible on a clear day and so it's easy to know where to jump in and start the dive.

The western side of the ship is home to a family of batfish that frequently joins divers on their dives. The middle section is mostly collapsed, but still interesting enough to dive.

There are a few nice features, the captain's cabin and steering wheel are mostly intact, and the hull is hollow, so sunlight plays in the darkness, giving you a good view of the inside. This is an excellent site for budding underwater photographers.

Batfish, giant hammour, snappers and the Arabian Angel fish are abundant. You might also see blennies and dottybacks hiding in the urchins, and barracuda and trevallies frequent this site. The collapsed deck and the hull are covered in clams, scallops, sponges, thorny oysters, sea squirts and barnacles, and hermit crabs, shrimp and gobie families can be seen on the sand around the wreck. A seahorse has been sighted near the bow of wreck in the seagrass area.

There's sometimes a moderate current and low visibility. Be sure to also dive with a Delayed Surface Marker Buoy (DSMB) so your dive boat can easily locate you when you need picking up.

Nearby to the Pearl wreck is also the Car Cemetery dive site.

Yellow-mouth moray eel

DIVES ON HOLD

While the developers of the offshore islands promise new dive sites, these old favourites are temporarily undiveable.

Some sites covered in earlier editions of this book, such as Rashid Wrecks and Jumeirah Artificial Reef, have been lost entirely due to construction work on the island projects. Others have been damaged, covered in silt, or lie in the path of construction shipping.

Hopefully, the sites detailed opposite will recover from the effects of nearby construction. However, the Cement Barge wreck, which we previously covered in detail, has now had its day. It's only about 10-11m deep, has a lot of silt build-up and the barge has deteriorated significantly. The wheel house has collapsed and the structure is breaking up.

To stay up-to-date on the conditions of dive sites, contact a local dive operator.

CAR BARGE & TUG

GPS
N25°16'16"
E55°08'02"

Depth: 20m
Distance from harbours:
DIMC 10.7nm @ 356°
DOSC 7.4nm @ 321°

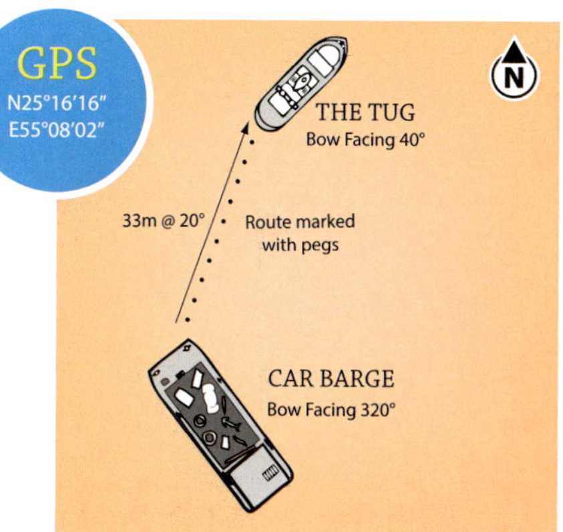

The barge, sunk in 1986, is still virtually intact and lies upright with her bow pointing north-west, at 320°. Her hold is filled with old cars, and there's a small wheelhouse and cabin on the stern. Her bow has a 33m-long row of pegs running to a tug that was used for harbour work.

Diving

If you swim into the barge's cabin the noise of your breathing will be masked and your bubbles hidden, so you'll find that any fish on the site will start to close in. There are sections of debris to the north of the barge that the more adventurous can explore. These two wrecks made for a good day dive and an excellent site at night, but are now heavily silted. The site is recovering, but not many divers visit.

MV SARRAF THREE

GPS
N25°16'07"
E55°07'55"

Depth: 20m
Distance from harbours:
DIMC 10.5nm @ 355°
DOSC 7.3nm @ 319°
Dubai Creek 8.8nm @ 267°

On the night of 30 April, 1981, the UAE coast was hit by a rare and fierce hailstorm. During the storm – in which golf ball-sized hailstones were recorded – the MV Sarraf was rammed by the MV Taiser while moored in Dubai. The Sarraf was raised that same year, re-floated and then abandoned in nearby Hamriya Port.

She was privately bought in August 1985 that same year, then taken out and sunk at her present location. She lies upright and virtually intact (minus her brass fittings), with her bow pointing towards the north.

Diving

Before the offshore construction work began to affect visibility and marine life, when diving on this wreck was recommended, the site featured numerous, colourful soft corals and was excellent for a night dive. It has recovered to some extent, but not many operators visit these days.

MUSANDAM

MUSANDAM:

DIVING THE FJORDS

Musandam has a rugged, isolated and beautiful coastline; the towering Hajar Mountains rise directly out of the sea creating spectacular fjord-like scenery. There are endless possibilities for divers, and sheltered bays perfect for snorkellers.

Adventurous and experienced divers will find lots of intriguing dive sites in this area. Visibility is usually good – up to about 20m. The dives are all on the east coast and easily accessible from the UAE by dhow or motorboat, often without the need to officially enter Oman. Sites such as Lima Rock and Octopus Rock are unmissable.

There's much more to see: the peninsula has a huge section of coastline, from Ras Al Khaimah in the north of the UAE, around Ras Musandam in the Strait of Hormuz, then down the east coast to Dibba, a small fishing village that's partly Emirati and partly Omani.

For divers there are two main ways to explore the area; either by boat up the east coast from Dibba or by driving to Khasab, the capital of Musandam. It's always advisable to take your diving qualifications and some form of identification with you.

Dibba

Dibba is partly in the UAE and partly in Oman. If you hire one of the dive boats or dhows operating from the east coast (from Dibba Bayah Harbour), you can enter Omani waters without crossing the border checkpoint. However, you're not allowed to land, and if the authorities approach you at sea you could be in trouble for not having a permit to enter Oman. Alternatively, book a trip (including dive gear) with an east coast dive operator.

To reach Dibba Bayah Harbour, in the Omani part of Dibba, go through the UAE part of town, and then cross the beachside border checkpoint with your passport. The harbour is 10 minutes from here.

Travellers on a UAE visit visa can cross the border with just their passport, but anyone with a UAE residence visa has to have a permit. Dive centres, hotels and tour operators can organise permits if you submit all paperwork to them in advance.

You will receive a heavy fine for carrying alcohol across the border, even if you have a liquor licence.

White Rock aka 'Sydney Opera House'

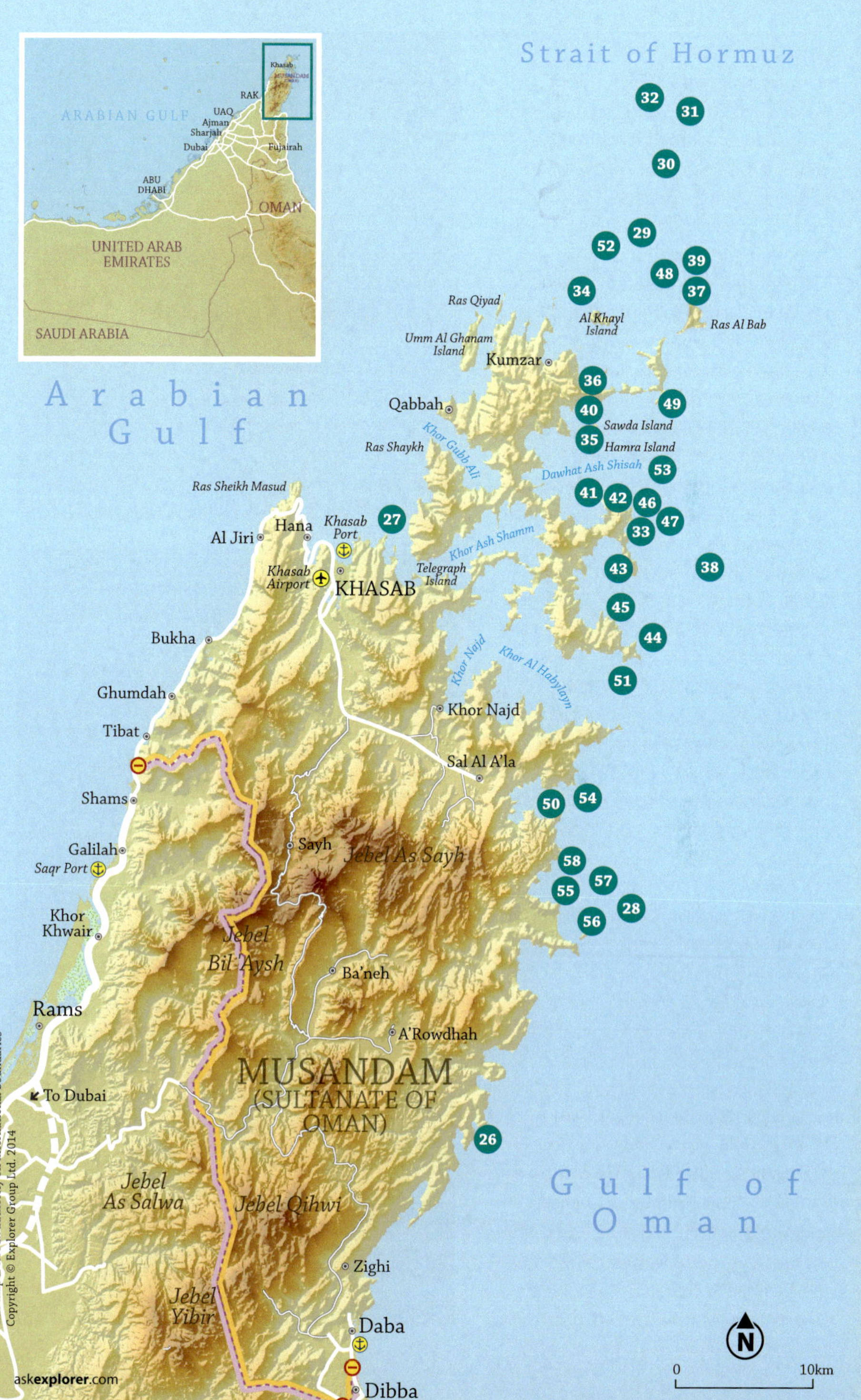
Strait of Hormuz
Arabian Gulf
Gulf of Oman
ARABIAN GULF
RAK
UAQ
Ajman
Sharjah
Dubai
Fujairah
ABU DHABI
OMAN
UNITED ARAB EMIRATES
SAUDI ARABIA
Khasab
MUSANDAM
Ras Qiyad
Umm Al Ghanam Island
Al Khayl Island
Ras Al Bab
Kumzar
Qabbah
Sawda Island
Hamra Island
Ras Shaykh
Khor Gubb Ali
Dawhat Ash Shisah
Ras Sheikh Masud
Hana
Khasab Port
Al Jiri
Khasab Airport
KHASAB
Telegraph Island
Khor Ash Shamm
Bukha
Khor Najd
Khor Al Habylayn
Ghumdah
Tibat
Sal Al A'la
Shams
Galilah
Saqr Port
Sayh
Jebel As Sayh
Khor Khwair
Jebel Bil Aysh
Ba'neh
Rams
A'Rowdhah
MUSANDAM (SULTANATE OF OMAN)
To Dubai
Jebel As Salwa
Jebel Qihwi
Zighi
Jebel Yibir
Daba
Dibba
0
10km
N
26 27 28 29 30 31 32 33 34 35 36 37 38 39 40 41 42 43 44 45 46 47 48 49 50 51 52 53 54 55 56 57 58
askexplorer.com
This map is not an authority on international boundaries
Copyright © Explorer Group Ltd. 2014

Khasab

The other option for exploring Musandam is to go overland to Khasab, via the west coast road through Ras Al Khaimah, and to contact one of the diving centres there (see the Dive Directory. You can take your own diving equipment with you, but dive tanks are sometimes refused entry, since the Omanis want to restrict diving to registered dive organisations.

To enter the Musandam Peninsula you will need a visa. Visa requirements depend on your nationality and whether you're a UAE resident or a visitor. Remember that regulations in this part of the world often change virtually overnight, so check details before you leave to avoid disappointment. There are UAE and Omani border posts at the entry point to Musandam, so visitors will need the correct UAE visa in order to return to the Emirates.

If you have UAE residency and are on List 1 or 2 (see opposite), a visa can be obtained on arrival at the border. If you are not on either list, or if you're on List 2 and a tourist in the UAE, you will need to apply for a visa at the Omani Embassy in Abu Dhabi (02 446 3333) or the Consulate in Dubai (04 397 1000). The fee is Dhs.50. Visas usually take one working day to process, although it is probably wise to allow three to four days.

If you want to visit Oman more than once, a multiple entry visa is available at the border (for List 1 nationalities) or in advance from your nearest Oman embassy or consulate (List 2). The cost is RO.10, and the visa is valid for one year. Your passport must be valid for not less than one year at the time of applying. Holders of this visa can stay for up to three weeks at a time, but a minimum of three weeks must elapse between each visit.

The local currency is the Omani Riyal (RO

Diving in Musandam

LIST 1

Europe: Andorra, Austria, Belgium, Croatia, Cyprus, Czech Republic, Denmark, Estonia, Finland, France, Germany, Greece, Hungary, Iceland, Ireland, Italy, Latvia, Liechtenstein, Lithuania, Macedonia, Malta, Moldova, Monaco, Luxembourg, Netherlands, Norway, Poland, Portugal, Romania, San Marino, Slovakia, Slovenia, Spain, Sweden, Switzerland, United Kingdom and Vatican
South America: Argentina, Bolivia, Brazil, Chile, Colombia, Ecuador, Paraguay, Suriname and Venezuela
Other Countries: Australia, Brunei Darussalam, Canada, French Ghana, Hong Kong, Indonesia, Japan, Lebanon, Malaysia, New Zealand, Seychelles, Singapore, South Africa, South Korea, Taiwan, Thailand, Turkey and United States

LIST 2

Albania, Belarus, Bosnia-Herzegovina, Bulgaria, China, Egypt, India, Iran, Jordan, Morocco, Russian Federation, Syria and Ukraine

or OR), which is divided into 1,000 baisa (or baiza). The exchange rate is about Dhs.10 = RO.1. Dirhams are widely accepted in Oman.

By car you can enter and exit Musandam on the Ras Al Khaimah side of the peninsula, or through Dibba on the east coast, but you can't drive from Khasab to Dibba through Wadi Bih as this road is only open to Omani nationals.

Night Diving

We have dived most of the sites mentioned in this area at night with great success. Less experienced divers may find the currents a greater problem at night than in the daytime.

For dhow trips, book ahead with the operators. Most professional dive centres will offer night dives, but might require a minimum amount of divers if you are using their speedboats. Musandam is a great location for night diving but proper training is required. Good advice is to use a UV light to enjoy the phosphorescence, coral and rays. (Operators are listed in the Directory.)

Arabian blue-striped dottyback

Operators

Most operators have dhows and speedboats, including Al Marsa Travel & Tourism & Charter who offer tailor-made charters; Sheesa Beach Travel and Tourism also offer trips for recreational and technical divers; and Nomad Ocean Adventures has packages for rec and tech divers, and has a guesthouse. Extra Divers in Khasab and in Zighy Bay has speedboat trips. All these centres are PADI or SSI and offer courses, equipment, and some offer nitrox or trimix gas blends.

Other operators not affiliated with dive-training agencies, such as Hormuzline, Khasab Travel & Tours, Musandam Sea Adventures and Rahal Musandam offer dhow or speedboat rental with dive gear but not always with dive guides. For contact information see Boat, Yacht & Dhow Charters in Further Info.

To take your own boat to Musandam, seek permission from the Omani Coastguard at Dibba Bayah Harbour coastguard post.

DIVER SAFETY

- Subscribe to dive insurance such as DAN. Dive centres' insurance only covers third party liability. Private insurance should cover transport and medical fees.
- Follow the dive plan given by the operator. Try to avoid diving without a dive guide or an experienced diver that knows the sites well and always stick with your buddy or dive group.
- Be aware that the currents, upward and downward, can be challenging for even the most experienced of divers. Operators here usually run drift dives. A reef hook can help you to cling to a wall. Don't hook coral and be wary of venomous fish along walls. Do not touch marine life.
- Use an SMB (Surface Marker Buoy) when diving in Musandam. Orange stands out best against the coastal rocks. Good advice is to carry a mirror or other means of attracting attention.

DIVE 26

THE CAVES

The entrance to The Caves

GPS
N25°48'14.4"
E56°22'03.0"

Depth: 10-18m | **Snorkelling:** Yes | **Night dive:** Yes
Other names: Khor Mala Caves, Sannat Caves
Distance from harbours:
Dibba Bayah Harbour 10.5nm @ 028°
Distance from other dive sites:
Lima Rock 9.9nm @ 212°
Ras Musandam 36.5nm @ 194°

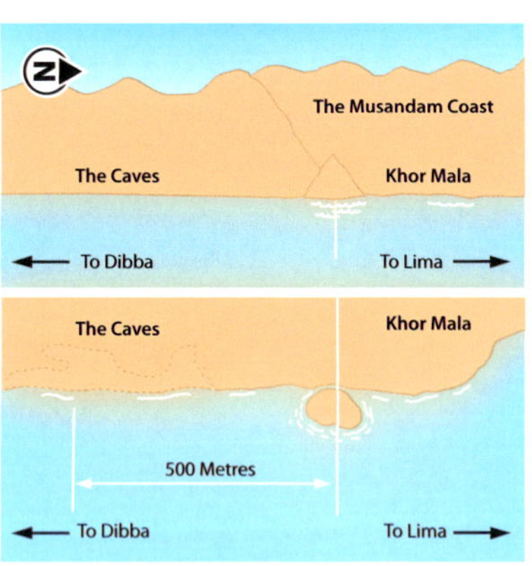

Great exploring and a wide variety of marine life awaits in these limestone caverns.

For interesting diving in underwater caverns, start either at 60m from the exit point at Ras Sannat, where a cave is visible from the surface, or go 500m from the pointed rock stack at Khor Mala, where you'll find the caves below the surface.

Erosion by the sea has cut these caves deep into the limestone rock face. The main chamber is an undercut section that runs about 15 to 20m into the rock. The bottom, at about 10m, is sandy and marked with boulders. There are several small recesses (at 18m) at the back of the main chamber.

Diving

This is a good third dive of the day as it's shallow and doesn't go too deep into the rock face. A bright torch is essential for seeing your way, especially as this is a great site for peeking into holes and tunnels in search of sheltering life.

It's also an excellent night dive. Look out for all the crustaceans coming out to feed. After dark it's a great opportunity to see stingrays, squid, lobsters and hunting lionfish. Octopus are also regularly spotted, as well turtles feeding on soft corals.

Snorkelling

Snorkelling here can be very good too. Swim along the rock wall and duck dive into the entrance of the cave – its roof is just above the surface of the water. A torch is necessary to make the most of this location and to see all the colours.

Marine Life

Enter slowly, looking for stingrays and resting sharks on the sandy bottom. As you move into the caves, large shoals of golden cardinal fish will form curtains of red and silver as they guard the deeper crevices. The caves attract many varieties of small fish seeking safety and food.

Cleaner shrimps hide in the hollows. These white- and brown-banded shrimps can usually be seen by their tentacles sticking out of their hiding places. If you're lucky, you may spot some spiny lobsters hiding deep in the cracks. At night, octopus and turtles rest on the bottom.

Shrimp

Burrfish

DIVE 27

THE LANDING CRAFT

GPS

N26°12'40.0"
E56°17'05.1"

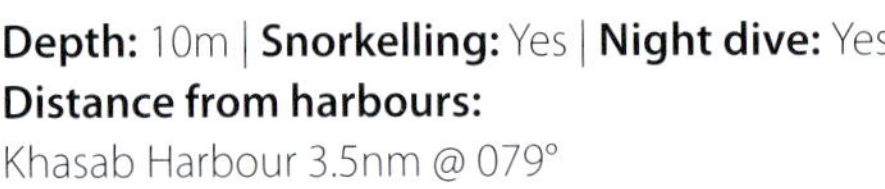

Depth: 10m | **Snorkelling:** Yes | **Night dive:** Yes
Distance from harbours:
Khasab Harbour 3.5nm @ 079°

A sheltered site that offers divers a chance to practise their wreck penetration skills.

This was a landing craft that specialised in carrying water to the villages that weren't able to receive water by road. The vessel was one of a fleet of three boats, each named after one of the villages they frequented with their essential load.

The hull of The Musandam split with age, and it was decided that the vessel would be decommissioned. There was also a light aircraft that had been at Khasab Airport for about two years and the decision was made to load the plane onto the landing craft and take them out to sea to be sunk.

Diving

This small vessel sits upright and intact on the seabed at just 10m, with its bow facing 20°. The Musandam has a well-preserved and undamaged wheelhouse, which is surprising given that it's only 3-4m from the surface, and you can swim in and out of it easily. On a past dive, a prankster placed the loo on top of the wheelhouse.

You will be able to see the engine room through gaps in the deck, but it's a very tight squeeze and entry is certainly not to be attempted without adequate training.

Another interesting feature is the

aeroplane laid out on the deck with its wings alongside. You can see the propellers and the cockpit area with petrol tanks underneath what's left of the seats. At the front of the vessel is the landing deck which seems to attract a plethora of fish life. You can also find small bits and pieces of debris and tyres strewn about the wreckage.

After looking for shrimps, crabs and blennies in all the nooks and crannies on the wreck, take a swim over to the edge of the reef and look in the staghorn corals. You're likely to find a citron goby city in every coral you peer into.

This is an ideal beginners' site on the edge of a protected bay with the rocky shoreline close by. It's only 15 minutes to the harbour, making it an easy night dive destination.

Snorkelling

Snorkellers will enjoy this site too, as it's relatively shallow and it's possible to see the wreckage from the surface most of the time.

Marine Life

As the wreck has been here for several years, you'll see many shells and a variety of hard corals on it; primarily brain and staghorn corals encrusted around anything they can find, such as the wreck's surfaces, along ropes, and clinging to the metal...

As Khasab isn't dived as much as other UAE sites, the fish appear to be quite unconcerned about divers and will swim almost into your face and regulator.

Yellow snappers are always in abundance, especially in and around the landing ramp area. You're also likely to spot a couple of clownfish and anemone colonies.

Safety

This is a good site for students thanks to its protected position. You still need to take the precautions you'd usually take when diving a wreck though, and watch that you and your equipment are not caught or cut on the rusty wreckage. It's also important that you wear protective gear.

Wreck register: Not charted
Name: The Musandam
Nationality: Unknown
Year built: Unknown
Type: Landing craft
Tonnage: Unknown
Dimensions: L: 35m, B: 7m, D: 3m
Cargo: None
Date sunk: 1990

WARNING

Do not attempt to enter the engine room without adequate training. There's also a lot of rubbish in the form of rusted cans and broken glass lying around here.

Diver in the wheelhouse

DIVE 28 LIMA ROCK

Squirrelfish in soft corals

GPS
N25°56'27.2"
E56°27'51.2"

Depth: 12-60m | **Snorkelling:** Yes | **Night dive:** Yes
Other names: Jazirat Lima, North and South Sides
Distance from harbours:
Dibba Bayah Harbour 20.3nm @ 029°

Boulders, limestone caverns, abundant reef life and a nearby island to chill out on.

A great dive! North of Dibba, Lima Rock, amid a plethora of coral and marine life, marks the southern entrance to Lima Bay. This small island is a pinnacle of limestone rock, about 800m long by 200m wide with steep, jagged sides. The waves have undercut the rock in places, leaving shallow caves and deep fissures. Sheer cliffs drop almost vertically to a depth of about 12m, then boulders and scree run steeply down to a sandy bottom at more than 60m. Check tides and expect currents, including downward currents.

Diving

The beauty of Lima Rock is that it can be dived in most weather and tidal conditions. If the sea is rough, or the current is running on one side, the other side is usually calm. Beware of the strong currents at the eastern and western tips of the island and carry a reef hook and SMB.

Snorkelling

Snorkellers will enjoy the site too and the north side of the island offers more shelter if you keep close to the rock face.

Eagle ray

Marine Life

On the southern side of the island, there are a couple of relatively deep caves, one of which used to be the home of a 2.5m nurse shark, now only seen very occasionally. At the south-eastern end of the island, a massive boulder guards the easternmost tip of the island. If the currents are mild, wait on this monolith and look out into the deep water for tuna, jacks, sharks and devil rays. You may even see a whale shark or a sunfish.

Between 12 and 20m, the boulder field is covered with hard corals (table, staghorn, brain and boulder coral), and patches of soft corals (orange and pink teddybear coral). The marine life is abundant, with large shoals of reef fish.

At 20m and deeper, abundant yellow and green coloured black coral, and numerous clumps of purple coral appear between the patches of sand. Look out for the yellow-mouthed morays with their vivid, colourful markings. Moving deeper towards the shelving sand, white tip sharks, marble rays, torpedo rays and leopard sharks are often seen resting on the bottom.

On the north side, steep walls drop down to the sand at 20m. This side of the island is in shade from mid morning onwards. Keep an eye open for critters and nudibranchs. They vary in size from 2mm to 20cm, and are very colourful.

The island is also home to a variety of birds such as ospreys, swifts and sooty falcons that frequent the high ramparts of the rock, making it an interesting location to wait between dives.

WHEN WAS THAT AGAIN?

If you haven't been diving in a while – which means for more than six months – it's highly recommended that you take a scuba review or refresher course. Most dive centres offer them and you'll enjoy your next dive more, knowing that your skills have been refreshed and revised.

MORE OF MUSANDAM

Moon wrasse

Since the last edition of this book, we've discovered several new sites in the Musandam area...

It's now easier than ever to dive the spectacular northern tip of Musandam, even the sites in the Strait of Hormuz. Several dive organisations and tour companies now operate in this area, offering magical trips.

The area is vast, and with its memorable scenery and many wonderful dives, it would take another book just to cover the Musandam Peninsula. Diving this area is very special, particularly as your chance of seeing many different types of sharks and larger fish is greater here than on other stretches of the coastline.

We have put together a selection of our favourite dive sites here, with a brief description of each. Over the years, the best sites have proven to be those around the islands, headlands and promontories. These rocky outcrops in the main current flow attract sharks, giant trevally, jacks, rays, shoals of tuna, dolphins and the occasional whale shark. The strong currents washing over the corals keep them bright, colourful and healthy. The bays and inlets like Khor Habalayn, though calmer in rough weather, usually have slightly poorer visibility and there is less chance of seeing the bigger species. However, this area has great camp sites and shallow reefs great for snorkelling.

The currents can be strong so try to plan your trips to include sites where you can shelter from the current when it's running.

DIVE 29
BU RASHID

GPS
N26°24'12.0"
E56°29'42.0"

Other Name: Rashid's Father, Tawakul
Depth: 6-40m+

One of the larger islands in the Strait of Hormuz. The steep rocky cliffs drop down to a coral-covered shelf at 6m and continue on down to a wide shelf at 25 to 30m before dropping on to the shelving sand at 40m. On the north side is a wreck of a small fibreglass boat, and several species of shark are regularly seen here. The eastern side is a carpet of soft coral, descending all the way to the sea floor. Best dived on slack tides due to the power of the current.

Leopard shark

DIVE 30
ENNERDALE ROCK

GPS
N26°27'39.5"
E56°30'57.2"

Depth: 16-50m+

This spectacular site is named after a bulk carrier that sank upon striking the rock. The rock, which is quite difficult to find – and to dive – is located in the main shipping channel where the currents can be fearsome, but the experience is well worth the effort.

The rock peak rises very steeply from the deep to a sharp point at 16m below the surface. We use a grappling hook on a shot line to get down to the rock, which glows out of the dark greenish-blue as you dive towards it.

The first things you'll see are the huge pelagics such as trevally and jacks that patrol the rock, and then myriad bright corals. The fish here are completely unafraid of divers and allow you to get very close. Remember not to try and touch any marine life, and keep your bearings at all times in the strong current.

Jack patrolling the reef

DIVE 31
FANAKU ISLAND

GPS
N26°29'55.1"
E56°31'50.4"

Other Name: Gap Island
Depth: 6-50m+

Fanaku Island is the middle of three islands in the centre of the Strait of Hormuz. It consists of sparsely covered rock walls that descend in terraces on the eastern side, and on the western side there are lovely areas with vibrant coloured soft corals. The currents can be very strong here and the island doesn't offer any shelter. This means that only the smallest and strongest of marine growth survives. This is shark, jack and tuna territory and they can be seen on most dives. Zebra sharks are common here between March and October.

Spotted sweetlips

DIVE 32
GREAT QUION ISLAND

GPS
N26°30'21.0"
E56°30'51.6"

Other Name: Salamah Island
Depth: 16-50m+

The largest of three islands, Great Quion offers protection from currents. The island's west side consists of gradually shelving rock, coral and sand.

From the northern point of the island, a submerged and narrow rocky ridge runs north east about 20m below the surface. Extending to 900m, this ridge drops very steeply to the west and is a hunting ground for sharks, trevally and jacks.

On the south eastern side, an underwater ridge runs in a southerly direction from 11m down to 30m+. Zebra sharks, rays, barracuda, trevally, milkfish and beautiful soft corals proliferate. This site may only be attempted by divers with extensive drift diving experience and those who are proficient in SMB deployment.

Arabian blue-striped dottyback

DIVE 33

HARD ROCK CAFE

GPS
N26°12'13.0"
E56°29'18.5"

Other Name: Corkscrew Rock, Ras Bashin, Temple Island, The Cube
Depth: 6-20m+

This rock pinnacle has a shallow side of large coral-covered boulders and patches of sand. Easiest is to start at the rock and swim back to the coast. You'll see huge shoals of reef fish, lots of coral and rays and sharks. If you start from the east side, following the wall and patch of sand, you'll find the wreck of a dhow. Following the wall further can take you very deep and you should not proceed unless you're trained in technical diving. This colourful site is good for snorkelling, too.

Snorkellers at Hard Rock Cafe

DIVE 34

JAZIRAT AL KHAYL

GPS
N26°22'24.0"
E56°26'51.0"

Other Name: Horse Island
Depth: 16-40m+

The deeper north side of this island is dived from the headland in the east into the bays, and along the north west headland. Steep cliffs and rock scree run sharply down into the sea to a coral covered shelf 6m deep. The boulder and coral slope steps down to a wide shelf at 25 to 30m, then drops on to the shelving sand at 40m. You'll see lots of reef fish here and perhaps even the occasional shark.

WARNING

Ear pain on ascent due to reverse block? (Too much air trapped in the ears.) Don't try to equalise. Descend slowly until the pain subsides and then try to ascend slowly.

DIVE 35
JAZIRAT HAMRA &

DIVE 36
JAZIRAT SAWDA

GPS
N26°16'54.0"
E56°27'12.0"

GPS
N26°17'43.6"
E56°27'12.5"

Other Name: Red Island and Black Island
Depth: 6-30m+

Jazirat Hamra (Red Island) and Jazirat Sawda (Black Island) lie inside the sheltered bay of Dawhat Ash Shisah (Sheesa Bay). A shallow shelving coral reef dotted with boulders surrounds both islands. The reef runs out into sand at a depth of 20m. Both sites teem with reef fish. Of the two sides, the east is dived more regularly. It's very popular for Discover Scuba Diving experiences and a great anchorage for an overnight safari, as there's a lovely little beach to have a bonfire or a barbecue.

Lionfish

DIVE 37
JAZIRAT MUSANDAM EAST HEAD

GPS
N26°22'11.0"
E56°32'18.0"

Other Name: Picnic Bay
Depth: 6-50m+

When the currents are strong and the sea is a little rough, this headland and bay offer calm water and superb diving. At the point of the headland to the east, the cliff wall drops straight down to a depth of 50m. If you follow this wall into the northern bay, it gradually becomes a very pretty gentle coral garden slope, where a frenzy of reef fish feed. Sharks and schools of eagle rays may be seen rounding the headland. Technical divers drop to 50m where you can see tiger and lemon sharks, as well as the occasional hammerhead.

Starfish

DIVE 38
JAZIRAT UMM AL FAYYARIN

GPS
N26°10'31.9"
E56°32'47.2"

Other Name: Mother of Mouse
Depth: 6-50m+

The south bay and the east side are the best dive sites on this island, but be aware of currents. Go when currents are mild or running south.

Descending to 50m from the south east corner is a rocky outcrop that separates its two dive sites. Hanging in the current are jacks, barracuda and tuna. The east side dive consists of a magnificent reef of staghorn and table coral, dropping in steps from six to 20m, from the rock to the northern end of the island. The south bay consists of fallen rock covered in coral that descends to a sandy slope at 20m. The sand continues downwards past 50m. Sunfish, huge schools of snapper, turtles, barracuda, large honeycomb moray eels, rays, sharks and nudibranchs can be seen here.

Coral descends down the slope

DIVE 39
KACHALU ISLAND

GPS
N26°23'45.5"
E56°31'48.1"

Other Name: Pop Rock
Depth: 6-40m+

A popular site, but with strong downward currents, so you should only dive with a guide who knows the site well. The island's rock walls drop straight down to a shelf at 5m, then descend in steep steps to more than 50m. One cave extends through the island and is nicknamed the 'washing machine' – for obvious reasons! The walls are characterised by gullies, holes and small shelves filled with hard and soft corals. There are large shoals of fish, plus rays, barracuda and sometimes, whale sharks.

Mushroom soft coral

DIVE 40
MUSHROOM ROCK

GPS
N26°17'20.39"
E56°27'4.38"

Depth: 5-25m

Inside Sheesa Bay between Red and Black Islands, the reef is flat-topped with sloping walls and an underwater ridge on the eastern side. There's an abundance of marine life including: fusiliers, barracuda, jacks, parrot fish, kingfish, stingrays, scorpionfish, batfish, damselfish and honeycomb eels. It's best dived on a slack high tide due to the current. You'll need a GPS or landmark triangulation to find it.

DIVE 41
RAS ALULL

GPS
N26°14'51.22"
E56°27'46.07"

Depth: 5-25m

Also inside Sheesa Bay, this is a sloping wall full of soft corals with barracuda, eagle rays, porcupinefish, jacks, stingrays, turtles, and sometimes leopard and white tip sharks. Enter at 4m, gradually descending to the corner, but be aware of current. There are some great coral pinnacles in the area too.

Soft corals

THE OL' FLY & DIVE

Combining diving and flying is always risky, so you should stop diving at least 24 hours before flying to give your body time to rehydrate and de-gas. Avoid long flights, and if you do drink alcohol during the flight you need to top up on even more water than usual to avoid becoming dehydrated. Better still, don't drink and dive!

DIVE 42
RAS AROUS

GPS
N26°14'23.12"
E56°28'51.67"

Depth: 5-25m

Ras Arous is also inside Sheesa Bay and comprises a beautiful slope with lots of soft corals. This area is similar to Ras Alull with lots of fusiliers, jacks, stingrays, turtles and eagle rays.

It's a sheltered site and so is suitable for all levels of experience.

If you've been diving elsewhere in the vicinity this makes for an excellent third dive of the day, or night dive if on an overnight safari. It is a sheltered site and the colourful corals give you the impression of diving in a garden. It's more of a macro dive with lots of small critters to be found. Visibility is usually between five and 15m.

Fan worm

DIVE 43
RAS BASHIN

GPS
N26°11'5.61"
E56°28'31.14"

Depth: 4-25m

Ras Bashin is at the northern headland of Shaboos Bay and it comprises a sandy bottom that becomes a sloping reef covered with a vast array of vibrantly coloured soft corals. There are always lots of reef fish darting around.

Start the dive with your right shoulder facing the reef (depending on the current) and dive towards the head of the bay. The regulars you should look out for include: batfish, butterflyfish, angelfish, mantis shrimp, eels and triggerfish. There are some beautiful corals at the point where the rock drops to 25m deep. Watch out for the pelagics cruising around as you round the point, especially early in the morning or towards dusk.

Clam

DIVE 44
RAS DILLAH

GPS
N26°07'51.0"
E56°29'16.2"

Depth: 6-40m+

This site runs 500m into the bay from the north headland tip at the entrance to Khor Habalayn. Dive starting inside the bay just before the headland and swimming around the corner in a northerly direction, or reverse the profile on an ebbing tide. Note that it's in shadow by late afternoon.

The sheer rock wall drops 15 to 20m to the sandy bottom, which is strewn with boulders. Follow the sand down and swim out a little, you'll reach a depth of 40m.

The rock walls and boulders are covered in black coral and the big pelagic fish tend to gather around the headland.

Sohal surgeonfish

DIVE 45
RAS DILLAH GHUBBAT ASH SHABUS BAY

GPS
N 26°08'37.3"
E 56°28'47.1"

Other Name: Lighthouse Rock
Depth: 6-30m+

A tall peak resembling a lighthouse dominates this cliff-walled bay. Ospreys perch high above the water surveying the dive boats. Rocks and boulders have tumbled down into the sea and onto steeply shelving sand at about 20m, and if you swim out the depth is more than 30m.

You may see feeding stingrays filtering the sand and causing sand storms. Undercutting of the rock walls and large boulders has created numerous overhangs and small caves (always good places to search for unusual marine life) while yellow and purple coral clings to the rocks. This is a colourful dive site with lots of large fish.

Purple coral

DIVE 46
RAS KHAYSAH SOUTH

GPS
N26°13'56.38"
E56°29'26.03"

Depth: 10-35m

This narrow rock promontory juts out into the sea for more than a kilometre, and lies diagonally across north and south running currents. If the current is strong on one side it is sheltered on the other (see Ras Kaysah North). It's best dived on a low tide, 200 to 300m from the point, and you start in about 16m of water. The terrain consists of cliff walls, boulders and coral at about 30m. You'll see sunfish, whale sharks, eels, wrasse, parrotfish, tuna and big-eye trevally. Drop in with your left shoulder to the reef and dive towards the eastern point. There is a sump in the middle of the dive; be careful here as the current creates a whirlpool effect.

DIVE 47
RAS KHAYSAH NORTH

GPS
N26°14'2.25"
E56°29'30.12"

Depth: 20-25m

The flipside of Ras Khaysah South, Ras Khaysah North is at the entry into Sheesa Bay. You'll find a gently sloping decorative coral wall, which descends down to a sandy bottom. Marine residents here include: cow tail rays, whip gobies, parrotfish, lionfish, snapper and angelfish. At the deepest point, around the headland, you can find rays, and trevally hunting in the current.

This site covers a large area, and it's sheltered, so it's a great option for diving when the currents are strong elsewhere. It's in shade in the morning, and well-lit by the afternoon.

DIVE 48
RAS MUSANDAM

GPS
N26°23'12.1"
E56°31'29.1"

Other Name: Wall Street
Depth: 6-50m+

This dive site is on the northernmost point of Jazirat Musandam, which is one of the largest islands in the area. The northern coast features high sheer cliffs that drop straight down into the sea to a narrow ledge at 6m, and then down to a wider shelf at 25 to 30m before reaching the shelving sand at 50m. Strong up and down currents make for an excellent drift dive for experienced divers. Sharks, dolphins, whale sharks, eagle rays, devil rays, giant trevallies and king barracudas are seen here. Enter from the south east and you can go with the current and swim along the reef which will be on your left side.

DIVE 49
RAS QABR AL HINDI

GPS
N26°18'33.8"
E56°30'52.1"

Other Name: Tip of the Indian Grave
Depth: 6m-30m+

This dive site extends from the easterly point of the peninsula, where the rocky bottom slopes down to the sand at 30m, to the south. The area is a carpet of velvety coral with the occasional rock or boulder sticking out. It's a stunning underwater garden, and it's worth searching the crevices to find smaller marine life hiding away.

Further south, the coral is not as abundant and the slope down to the sand is more gradual, with patches of sand starting at 10 m. Rays and white tip reef sharks are often seen cruising around here.

DIVE 50
RAS SAMID

GPS
N26° 1'33.19"
E56°25'33.13"

Depth: 5-15m

This site has a sloping coral reef down to a sandy bottom where you can see shoals of barracuda and fusiliers, batfish, cuttlefish, lobsters and turtles.

There are beautiful soft corals. To get the best view, start your dive entry from the interior of the bay and swim east towards Ras Samid.

Ras Samid is in Khor Qabal and drops off to 30m. Be wary of the fishing net in the area, though it does attract quite a lot of marine life. This is a calm area to dive, but bear in mind that this is not a very popular site as the military base is quite close.

Boxfish

DIVE 51
RAS SARKAN

GPS
N26°05'17.3"
E56°28'18.7"

Depth: 6-50m+

This dive site is around the headland on the south entrance to Khor Habalayn. The direction of the current will decide which side you will dive – but both are good. The site consists of fallen rock and coral with patches of sand below 20m. Try to make your way to the point of the headland and watch the trevally and tuna feeding in the main current stream. Whale sharks also like to visit here.

A dhow sank here years ago and it's still on the sand at 50m, making a great site for technical divers. Schools of devil rays are also regularly encountered on this site as well as the rare but amazing sunfish (also known as mola mola). Also watch for the cleaning stations, where large fish wait for smaller cousins to pick off their parasites.

Whale shark

DIVE 52
RUQQ SUWAYK

GPS
N26°24'11.9"
E56°28'42.1"

Other Name: Calculator Rock
Depth: 6-50m+

This seamount or submarine mountain can be seen just below the surface of the water at 6m. The top of the mount is flat and covered with soft corals. Several gullies cut into the top of the rock and the sides step down in terraces to a depth of over 50m.

On the west side of the mount, you'll find a trail of debris, consisting of cargo (including calculators) from a wrecked dhow that lies at 40m. Several types of shark can be seen here gliding up out of the depths or just circling the seamount.

Purple coral

DIVE 53
WHITE ROCK

GPS
N26°14'11.9"
E56°29'42.6"

Other Name: Sydney Opera House
Depth: 6-50m+

White Rock is a small island 500m to the north east of the Ras Khaysah promontory. The rocky sides of the island drop steeply down to depths of more than 50m. It's a small island and can easily be circumnavigated in a dive, and snorkellers will enjoy it too. The sides are characterised by small shelves and fissures. Patches of coral nestle in these clefts and cracks and the smaller marine creatures cling to the shelter they find here. There are always large shoals of fish patrolling the island's outer boundaries.

There's more marine life on the northern sides as opposed to the south side. This is a great site to dive if you have access to a DPV (Diver Propulsion Vehicle).

HEAVY METAL

The high temperatures, humidity and salinity of the Gulf mean that your dive gear will take a bit more strain than in other parts of the world. It's essential that you have your cylinders visually inspected once a year, and hydro-tested every five years.

HITCHHIKERS

Porcelain crab hitching a ride on a jellyfish

A juvenile filefish tags along

Many juvenile marine creatures take shelter in the tentacles of a jellyfish, possibly for safety and the chance of any food scraps. It's not clear how they are immune to the jelly's sting though.

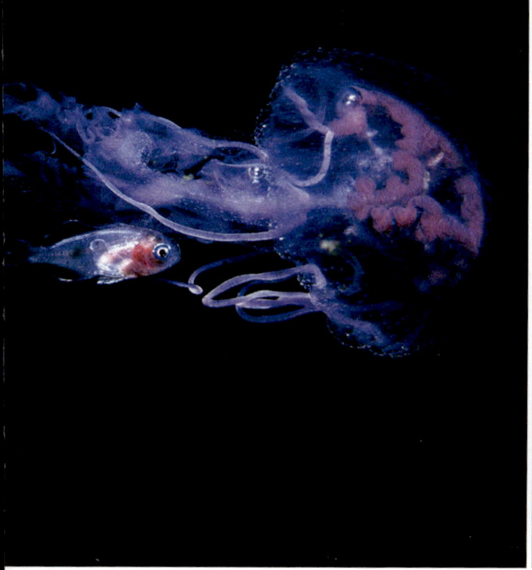

Porcelain crab hitching a ride on a jellyfish

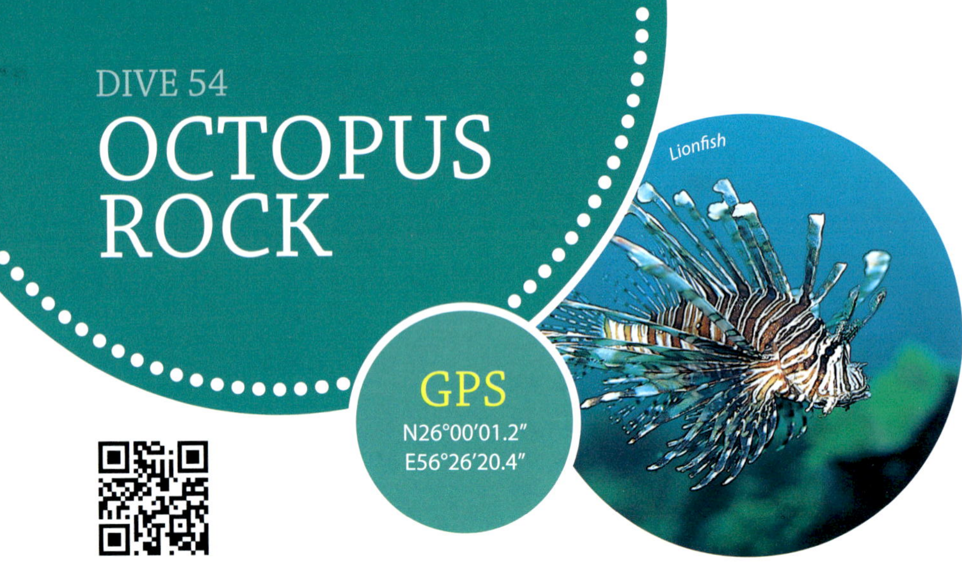

DIVE 54

OCTOPUS ROCK

GPS
N26°00'01.2"
E56°26'20.4"

Depth: 5-20m | **Snorkelling:** Yes | **Night dive:** Yes
Other Name: The Stack
Distance from harbours:
Dibba Bayah Harbour 23nm @ 022°

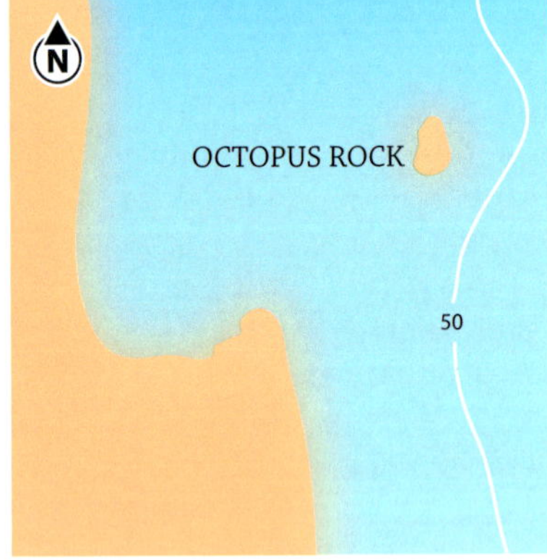

Another great Musandam dive, this site is practically a marine zoo.

With its distinctive undercut top, this isolated stack lies 3km offshore, north of Lima. It's about 50m in diameter and its sides drop vertically to a mixed rock and sand seabed. The rocky bottom runs in ridges to the west, north and east, forming sandy-bottomed gullies. The depth of these gullies varies from 15-20m around the base of the rock, when they slope off to the southeast, descending more than 50m.

Diving

Octopus Rock is a marine zoo that can be enjoyed in most weather and tidal conditions, thanks to its sheltered location in Lima Bay. After reaching the bottom, swim north from the base of the rock and you'll reach a rocky cliff that runs east to west. This leads to the gullies, which are a continuation of the cliff. Most divers turn back at the cliff and circle around the terraces of rock that surround the stack. If you continue, take note of your bearings; you can end up a long way from the rock.

Snorkelling

Snorkelling is very good, especially around the stack. To make the most of this site you will have to duck dive down the sides of the stack. Alternatively, you can swim away from the stack to the north-west. There are large outcrops of rock five to 8m from the surface that are always alive with reef fish.

Marine Life

The Stack is a gathering point for a great variety of shoaling fish life. Close to the rock you'll find numerous reef fish, while further out are jacks, trevally, tuna, barracuda and, if you're lucky, rays, sharks and huge nudibranchs. Seahorses can be seen on the tip of the eastern ridge at about 28m.

Soft and hard corals abound; green coloured black coral and purple soft coral whips predominate, and together with the pink and orange teddybear corals, they create a kaleidoscope of colour.

Pineapple fish

The rocks are home to fanworms, featherstars, juvenile crayfish and anemones. Look under overhangs and in hollows for black or red lionfish, but take care as these fish are poisonous. Stingrays can be seen feeding in the sand or resting under boulder coral overhangs. You also have a good chance of seeing leopard sharks, whale sharks, torpedo rays, devil rays, eagle rays and schools of yellow tail barracudas on this site.

WATCH YOUR BACK

When you go snorkelling, you need to keep your skin protected from the sun – because you're in the water you often don't realise you're burning until it's way too late. Wearing a t-shirt isn't enough: it doesn't block out UV rays. You can wear a 0.5mm wetsuit or a shortie, or at the very least a rash vest. Whatever you choose, make sure you supplement it with plenty of waterproof sunblock, especially on your neck, ears, and the backs of your legs – and keep hydrated.

Leopard shark

DIVE 55

PEARL ISLAND

GPS

N25°57'36.6"
E56°25'51.9"

Depth: 5-12m | **Snorkelling:** Yes | **Night dive:** Yes
Other Name: Oakley Island
Distance from harbours:
Dibba Bayah Harbour 20.6nm @ 031°
Distance from other dive site:
Lima Rock 2.2nm @ 303°

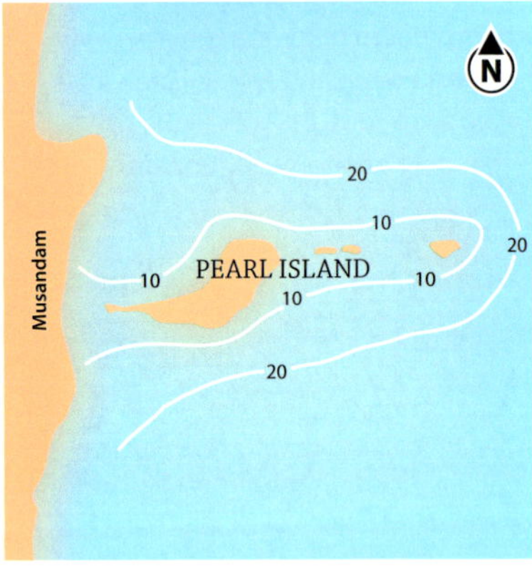

A great choice for a second dive of the day, this little gem offers snorkellers and divers plenty to see.

Located in Lima Bay, Pearl Island lies close to shore, just north of Lima. The water off the east tip of this rocky island is about 12m deep, and it gradually becomes shallower over the sand bar on the west side. Coral reef surrounds most of the island, descending gently from a depth of 5m to a sandy bottom at about 12m.

Diving

Since it takes about 50-60 minutes to swim around the island, and because of its depth, this site makes a good second dive with plenty to see. Corals run most of the way around the island and two rocks break the surface nearby. There's always a great variety of reef life here.

Snorkelling

The waters are usually very calm, making this a superb snorkelling site.

Marine Life

The reef is a mixture of hard and soft corals, with boulder, brain, cauliflower and daisy coral being the predominant hard corals, along with some orange and pink teddybear coral.

Blue-tail boxfish

The island attracts a huge variety of small reef fish, and at certain times of the year, great colonies of murex shells can be seen mating and laying their straw-like eggs.

The first thing you'll hear as you submerge are the parrotfish crunching the coral. As you approach these pink, blue and green pastel coloured fish, they swim off leaving a trail of coral particles.

There are several patches of anemones dotted around the island, and almost each one is attended by its resident clownfish. If you're wearing brightly coloured gloves, especially yellow, and wave them near these little clowns they'll probably try to attack. The assaults are usually harmless (although for a small fish, they can deliver a nasty bite), and the fish soon tire of the fun and return to the safety of their poisonous hosts.

PROTECT THE ENVIRONMENT-

Marine life can be easily damaged if you touch it, or pollute the water. The latest research shows that suncreams that are manufactured using nanotechnology (creams with smaller, more easily absorbed particles) are damaging to coral reefs because these particles break down in the water to form harmful substances. So try to avoid slathering on tons of cream right before a dive; put it on at least an hour before entering the water, or use thicker creams that sit on the skin.

It's also important to maintain neutral buoyancy so you're not crashing into the coral, and tuck away stray hoses and cables so they don't drag.

Never feed marine animals as you will disrupt the natural eco-system, and don't take anything away (such as shells) except any rubbish you may find.

DIVE 56

RAS HAMRA

GPS
N25°55'20.7"
E56°26'38.7"

Depth: 5-16m | **Snorkelling:** Yes | **Night dive:** Yes
Other Name: Ras Sanut, Wonder Wall, Purple Haze
Distance from harbours:
Dibba Bayah Harbour 20.4nm @ 028°

A shallow, colourful site with plenty of marine life, that's best dived in the early hours of the morning.

This site starts at the point of Ras Hamra and runs west along the north cliff face. It's a north-facing site and lies in shade by the early afternoon, so to see this coral wonderland, dive early in the morning.

Several large boulders break the surface near the headland, and the rest of the terrain consists of fallen rock and coral reef that drops to a sandy bottom.

The boulder coral on this site is extensive, running along the side of the cliff from 5m down to 16m, where the coral reef runs down to the sandy bottom.

Every gap is filled with corals, from brain and daisy to tables of staghorn and great clumps of cauliflower coral fighting for space between the boulder coral.

Diving

This is a shallow site with corals covering most of the fallen rocks down to a depth of 35m. When diving in these areas of hard coral, the sound of crunching fills your ears as the parrotfish munch away.

If you start the dive from the reef and keep heading south you will reach a sand plateau at 45m full of soft corals. This spot is a favourite cleaning station for sunfish.

Feather star

Snorkelling

This is an excellent site for snorkellers, as the reef starts at 5m, and you can see as much, if not more, than divers. Duck dive down and explore the corals, or simply drift over the reef and admire the display below.

Marine Life

This is a good site for reef fish as there are lots of hollows and gaps where the fish dart in and out, playing hide and seek. You'll often see turtles resting between the clumps of coral.

Look into dark holes for the red striped squirrelfish that tend to wait in shoals under the overhangs and in dark corners of the coral. Little fish, with big eyes, they like to stay in the safety of the shadows.

Deeper in the water there are several species of grouper; some are brown with blue spots, others are red with blue spots.

Gliding over the tops of the corals are the real dandies of the reef; emperor angelfish, butterflyfish and bannerfish. Meanwhile, boxfish propel themselves like miniature hovercraft from one gap in the coral to the next. Then there are the solitary beauties such as the Picasso triggerfish.

You will also find crown of thorns starfish grazing on the coral. When these voracious predators move on, they leave behind the bleached white skeletons of their former hosts. The site is also bursting with purple gorgons – hence the name, 'Purple Haze'.

WHEN THAT LAST DIVE WAS A WHILE AGO

If you haven't been diving for more than six months, it's highly recommended that you take a scuba review or refresher course. Most dive centres offer them and you'll enjoy your next dive more, knowing that your skills have been refreshed and revised.

Clownfish and anemone host

DIVE 57

RAS LIMA

Depth: 5-45m | **Snorkelling:** Yes | **Night dive:** Yes
Distance from harbours:
Dibba Bayah Harbour 18.8nm @ 028°

Two sites for the price of one – and double the enjoyment for snorkellers and divers.

The Ras Lima headland has two good dive sites for you to choose from; the north-facing site in Lima Bay and the east bay just south of the headland.

The north site is an interesting wall dive, with a steep cliff face that drops down to 10-15m in a tangle of fallen boulders. The east bay is located under the east headland cliffs. These are nearly vertical and plunge into the water to a depth of 6-8m where the coral reef gently runs down to the sand at 15m plus. Scattered throughout both sites are a number of large rocks, some of which form shallow caves.

Diving

The sites are in shadow in the afternoon, so plan to dive this site earlier in the day. Both locations can be explored in one trip, but it may be better to investigate each area separately. The headland divides the two sites, so if the tide and currents are running on one side, the other should be calm.

Whichever dive you do first, go down to the edge of the corals and the sand, then work around the bay to the headland. When the currents are mild, you can swim to the point of the headland and watch the shoals of larger ocean fish waiting to pounce on the reef fish. Close to the shore, on the east bay, are some large boulder coral heads with undercuts and hollows.

Snorkelling

The east bay is an excellent site for snorkellers, with coral starting at 5m and some large boulders breaking the surface close to the shoreline. The boulders offer varied terrain and are in easy reach of all levels of ability. The north side of Ras Lima should only be attempted by more experienced snorkellers.

Marine Life

This is a good site for smaller reef fish and big pelagic fish. Devil rays have been seen here on several occasions, and the area is probably a cleaning station for them. Seahorses can also be found amongst the black corals.

From five to 15m, corals cover most of the boulders that have fallen from the cliffs above. The boulder corals are large, with lots of cavities that make a perfect hideaway for fish like the blue triggerfish. Triggerfish don't seem to mind leaving parts of their bodies exposed when they are hiding, and you can often see bits of those distinctive, bright blue tails protruding from their hideaways when you're swimming overhead.

Batfish

Feather star in purple coral

Stag and table coral fill the gaps between the boulder coral, but as you go deeper, teddybear and purple corals start to take over. At 12 to 16m you'll find yellow-coloured black coral.

DIVE WITH A TORCH

As you know, red is the first colour to disappear as you descend below 9m. Some divers only think to take a torch with them if they're diving on a wreck, a cave or planning a night dive. But we take a torch with us all the time: when you see a coral, turn on the light and see all the colour appear before you – like magic!

DIVE 58

RAS MAROVI

GPS
N25°59'4.26"
E56°26'6.68"

Depth: 6-35m | **Snorkelling:** Yes | **Night dive:** Yes
Distance from harbours:
Dibba Bayah Harbour 21nm @ 024°

These islands and channels make for a fun drift dive when the tide is running.

RAS MAROVI

N

A collection of four islands make up Ras Marovi. The two larger islands run in a line south-east from the mainland of Jebel Al Khatamah. The first large island is separated from the mainland by a 100m channel and the second large island has a 200m channel dividing it from the first island. The two smaller islands run south from the most seaward island. The cliffs of the two larger islands drop down vertically into the water. On the north face of the inner island, the wall is sheer all the way down to 30m. The west coast of the seaward island is a beautiful sloping coral reef, which serves as a cleaning station for visiting fish. It's a great site for the third dive of the day, or a night dive. The coral garden slope and the cavern with its resident cowtail stingray are highlights.

Diving

The best diving is in the two channels. The depth of the channel nearest the shore varies from 30m to the north, rising up to 6m, and then dropping off to 28m in the south. The shallowest point of the second channel is 18m, dropping to over 30m on either side. The rocks and boulders slope down to a sandy bottom with a covering of both hard and soft corals. When the currents are running, drift dives through the channels can be great fun.

Start your dive at the north side of the seaward island and go with the current from the north, either on the left or right of the reef. You'll find seahorses, eagle rays, scorpionfish, barracuda, angelfish, parrotfish, nudibranchs, snapper, triggerfish, lionfish, eels and whale sharks.

The second larger isle (closest to the shore) can be one of the best dives of Musandam. If you start from the southern tip and keep following the sand bank you will eventually reach an underwater mount covered in black corals at 32m. Schools of yellow snappers, and yellow tail barracudas can be seen here as well as seahorses and nudibranchs. If you go around the mount, keeping the sand bank on your right side and the reef on your left side, you will eventually reach a much shallower plateau of lettuce corals, which is fantastic place for your safety stop.

Snorkelling

Swim round the edges of the islands. At the deeper points you may see sharks gliding beneath you. The two smaller islands are great for seeing large shoals of fish, but it's well worth duck diving down.

Octopus

Marine Life

There are lots of soft corals on these sites, including plenty of orange, pink and red teddybear coral. Purple and yellow coloured black coral is also prevalent. Soft lettuce coral is also abundant, and turtles come to feed and mate here.

The islands attract a lot of reef and pelagic fish. In the rock walls there are several shallow caves where large hammour lie in wait for their prey. Leopard sharks, zebra sharks, grey reef and white-tipped reef sharks and dolphins are regular visitors, while deeper down, stingrays rest on the sandy bottom. There have been several sightings of manta rays around the outer island.

Dolphin

EAST COAST

EAST COAST:

REEFS, WRECKS & ROCKY ISLANDS

Diving on the east coast is a very different experience to diving in the Arabian Gulf; while the west coast offers wrecks, the east coast is the place for divers seeking tropical marine life. However, the east coast does boast three great wrecks of its own – Inchcape, Inchcape 2 and Inchcape 10.

The east coast is affected by currents from the Gulf of Oman, the Arabian Sea and the Indian Ocean. These bring a multitude of exotic fish, and most resident divers in the UAE would agree that the greater diversity of marine life makes this the most interesting side of the peninsula to dive. Depending on the moon's cycle, currents can sometimes be a problem, and dive operators will either anchor or carry out drift dives. The visibility is normally between three and 20m.

Night Diving

Night diving on the east coast is very rewarding as there's plenty of marine activity once the sun goes down. At this time, a lot of creatures that are shy and sensitive to light come out to play, and to hunt and feed. Other creatures tuck themselves into rock crevices, hide in shells or cocoon themselves in a thin, filmy 'blanket' to guard against being eaten while they sleep.

At night, many creatures also change colour and turn various shades of red in an attempt to camouflage themselves (the most difficult colour to see underwater at night is red). When you find one of these creatures and shine your torch on them, you'll see their true beauty. This amazing transformation applies to many species of fish and octopus.

It's advisable that you receive adequate training before your first night dive. It's also a good idea to dive with a minimum of three torches between two divers (ideally two torches each). Ensure you grease the rings correctly (if appropriate) and always use alkaline batteries for safety. Batteries never seem to last long underwater and torches are prone to flooding, so it's wise to be prepared for the eventuality.

DIVER SAFETY

In order to make your east coast dives safe and pleasant, keep in mind the following points.

- If it's your first time on the site and you do not have a dive guide, follow the dive operator's recommended dive plan.
- Wear protective clothing for protection from the stinging hydrocorals found at some sites.
- At certain times of year there are small invasions of jellyfish – not all are of the stinging variety, but avoid finding out which are the hard way!
- Take a torch on the deeper dives. On sites like Coral Gardens, Anemone Gardens and Car Cemetery, the extra light will help you see the true colours underwater. And, of course, should you lose your dive buddy, the torch can be used for signalling.
- At many sites, especially Car Cemetery, you need to be aware of your buoyancy. This site in particular tends to silt up quickly, so control your finning techniques to minimise stirring up silt and clouding the water.

OMAN
Daba Bayah Harbour
Daba
Dibba
Dibba Al Hisn Harbour
Dibba
Al Fujairah
63
Dadna
RAK
65
Aqa'a
75
74
Snoopy Island
UNITED
ARAB EMIRATES
Bidiyah
60
Gulf of
Oman
Lulaya
Harbour
Khorfakkan
73
61
59
Khorfakkan
Port
64
66
69
71
72
To Dubai
Sharjah
Masafi
OMAN
Nahwa
UAE
Murba
70
Qurayya
Fujairah
Oil Terminal
68
Fujairah Port
FUJAIRAH
Fujairah
Intl Marine
Club
67
Fujairah
Intl Airport
62
Kalba
Khor Kalba
0
10km
N
ARABIAN GULF
Khasab
RAK
UAQ
Ajman
Sharjah
Dubai
Fujairah
ABU
DHABI
OMAN
UNITED ARAB
EMIRATES
SAUDI ARABIA
This map is not an authority on international boundaries
Copyright © Explorer Group Ltd. 2014

DIVE 59

ANEMONE GARDENS

GPS
N25°21'01.3"
E56°22'46.9"

Depth: 20m | **Snorkelling:** Yes | **Night dive:** Yes
Distance from harbours:
Lulaya Harbour 2.7nm @ 179°
Khor Fakkan Harbour 0.9nm @ 081°

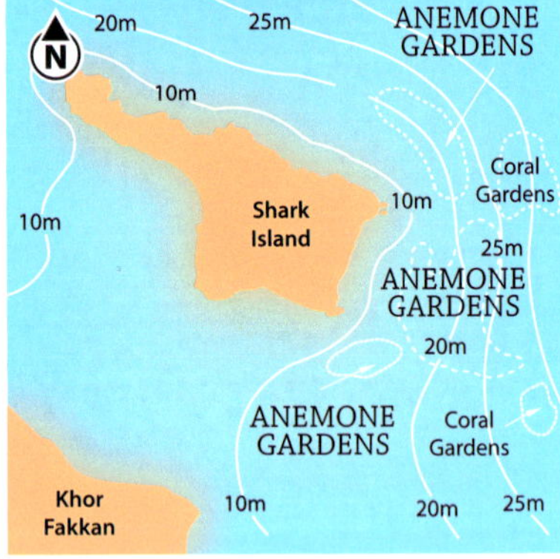

A beautiful site that makes a memorable dive, especially if you get to see a beautiful and elusive seahorse.

There are many small sites within Anemone Gardens which is a soft coral reef on a sandy seabed, located northeast of Shark Island. You'll find a few metres of depth variation but it's fairly level. These sites are particularly pretty with plenty of green whip coral (which is actually a type of black coral).

Diving

The best way to dive this area is with a compass and computer. Keeping an eye on your bottom time, explore the dive site and search for the elusive seahorses that can occasionally be found here. Make your way back to Shark Island and as the reef becomes shallower you can have a safety stop, extend your dive time and admire the spectacular marine life.

The site is even more beautiful at night. The corals appear brighter by torchlight, and they will have their tentacles or polyps fully extended for feeding. If you're lucky, you may even see those seahorses with their tails wrapped around the corals, but you'll have to look closely because they blend in almost perfectly with their surroundings.

Seahorse

Marine Life

Shoals of several species of fish congregate around the island – from jacks and juvenile barracuda to fusiliers and small schools of squid. You will find hard and soft coral in a kaleidoscope of colours, especially orange and red teddybear corals. Wispy green whip corals sway in the current.

This is an excellent dive spot that offers divers an opportunity to spot a shy seahorse – search carefully but if you find them *please do not touch*.

DIVE WITH A TORCH

As you know, red is the first colour to disappear as you descend below 9m. Some divers only think to take a torch with them if they're diving on a wreck, a cave or planning a night dive. But we take a torch with us all the time: when you see a coral, turn on the light and see all the colours appear before you – like magic!

At night you're also likely to see moray eels swimming about in their search for food and, if you look up, you may even see squid. Squid are very inquisitive and are attracted to light – they sometimes become dazzled and swim directly into the torch beam.

At night it's particularly difficult to locate the anchor line for your ascent, so extra care needs to be taken. Always be aware of your depth, take a compass bearing and keep to the dive operator's recommended dive plan and time. The dive master needs to be vigilant too. It's best to anchor between Anemone Gardens and Shark Island, otherwise your time underwater will be further limited due to depth.

Snorkelling

Snorkelling is possible, especially on days when the visibility is 20m or greater. But it's probably better to swim across to Shark Island (p.136) instead.

Squid

DIVE 60

CAR CEMETERY

Nudibranch

GPS

N25°25'07.0"
E56°22'34.2"

Depth: 18m | **Snorkelling:** No | **Night dive:** Yes
Distance from harbours:
Luyala Harbour 1.6nm @ 024°

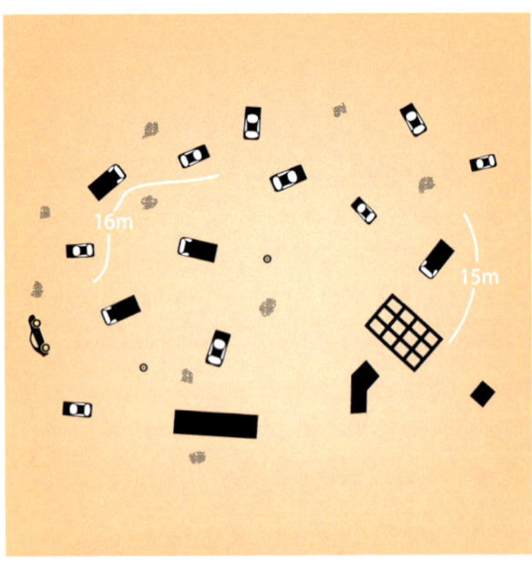

A site to test your navigation skills – with the reward of some unusual marine life.

Car Cemetery is a graveyard for wrecked cars that was created in about 1988 to form an artificial reef and a special site for fishing. There were about 200 vehicles here but following Cyclone Gonu in 2007 the number is more like 50, and the nucleus of the site covers an area of about 60 square metres. Note that the map above only depicts the main cluster of car wrecks.

Diving

Due to the flat seabed and the lack of any distinguishing features on the car, this is a difficult site, both to find and to navigate around. Visibility is also usually poor as the site is located near a wadi entrance.

There's also a lot of sediment in the area, so take care to keep your buoyancy in check, otherwise you will be down to zero visibility! In the daytime, you tend to meander from one wrecked car to another, looking in the distance for the shadow of the next vehicle. At night though, you won't be able to do this and you'll need to rely on your compass.

Although not frequently dived in the dark, Car Cemetery makes a memorable night dive. Corals come out at night

Whip goby on coral

extending their polyps to catch and feed on micro-planktons. We've encountered several unusual and light-sensitive nudibranchs that aren't seen in the daytime. There's also a beautiful sand anemone that we've seen at this site. During the day it's nondescript and looks a bit like half a tennis ball, but at night it extends itself to feed and resembles a head of celery decorated with baubles. Once a photo is taken, the bright flash from the strobe forces it to retract.

Due to the openness of the area, which is at the mercy of the wind and currents, this is a tricky site to navigate around at night, but it's not impossible. You will need to arrive in daylight and position yourself correctly, then wait for darkness. The dive operator should be prepared to up-anchor to collect you, as it's likely that you'll struggle to find the anchor rope for your ascent.

Marine Life

Most of the cars are covered with algae and fishing nets, some of which have fishing pots on them. Since the visibility is usually poor, it's best to take your time and look for smaller creatures, such as shrimps and Omani clingfish hiding among the featherstars. This site is considered a nudibranch haven and you'll find numerous species on the wrecks and discarded fishing nets.

Look carefully for seahorses and frogfish, as well as small manta rays and the occasional spotted eagle ray. There are also two large resident honeycomb morays that measure about 2m each on these wrecks.

Don't dismiss this site because of the low visibility; persevere, look closely, and you never know what you might find.

Honeycomb moray eel

DIVE 61

CORAL GARDENS

GPS
N25°21'12.0"
E56°22'48.0"

Depth: 26m | **Snorkelling:** No | **Night dive:** Yes
Distance from harbours:
Lulaya Harbour 2.6nm @ 179°
Khor Fakkan Harbour 1.1nm @ 081°

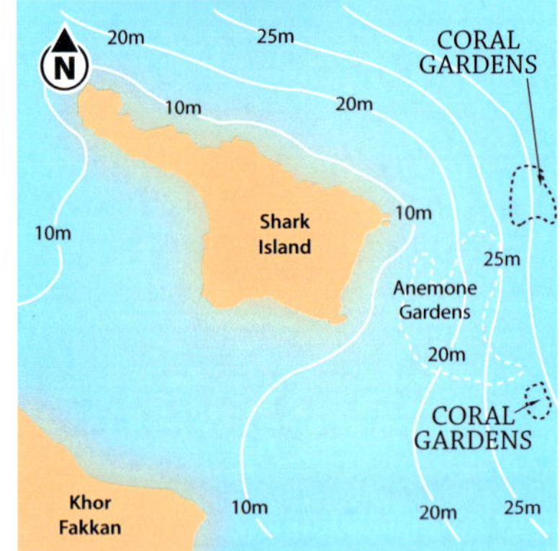

Resplendent with colourful corals, this is a great night dive for experienced divers.

Coral Gardens is one of the deepest sites on the east coast and can be an interesting multi-level dive. It consists of a soft coral reef on a sandy seabed and it's located on the north-eastern side of Shark Island.

The gardens are difficult to pinpoint unless you follow the correct bearings closely, but if you miss the exact location, don't worry; simply follow the compass bearing back to Shark Island and you'll encounter smaller, shallower reefs on the way that are full of interesting features. The area is resplendent with green coloured black whip coral.

Diving

As this is a 'flat' site, we suggest that you follow one of the following two dive plans (opposite), preferably with a dive computer. The site is prone to both thermoclines and unusually strong currents. Do not attempt Dive Plan 2 if there's a strong current running. We also suggest that this site is only suitable for more advanced divers with a minimum of 30 dives behind them.

Coral Gardens is a beautiful night dive. The corals are out feeding, nudibranchs are hunting, and molluscs, crayfish and crabs are on the march at an incredible speed. It's fascinating.

However, this is a deep night dive and fairly 'open', so adequate preparations and planning are vital. It's imperative that you take the time and depth into consideration and decide on contingency plans prior to your dive. Finding the anchor at night is tricky, but not impossible. In case of difficulty, you could navigate your way over to Shark Island, or surface slowly, shining your torch up towards the surface.

Citron goby

Snorkelling

Coral Gardens is too deep for snorkellers – instead head over to Shark Island.

Marine Life

This location has some unusual soft corals that we haven't seen on other dives. In particular, the delicate soft dandelion coral is fairly common here, as well as clumps of green wispy whip coral.

Shrimp on a starfish

During the winter months, you could be lucky enough to see razorfish (also known as shrimpfish), swimming upside down and darting from one clump of coral to another. You may also see guitar sharks, and large crocodilefish, with their big flat heads, crocodile shaped mouths and beautiful eyes with frilly eyelids. Seahorses are seen here occasionally, but they are becoming increasingly rare.

DIVE PLAN 1

Stay on the dive site proper, but watch your bottom time and give yourself a good safety stop. This is the plan to follow when the current is strong.

DIVE PLAN 2

For a multi-level dive, explore this site for a maximum of 10-15 minutes (or according to your dive computer), then follow a compass bearing back to Shark Island. You'll find that your bottom time increases as you follow the reef up to 13m and arrive at the base of the island, usually within 30 minutes. This allows you more time to enjoy the site, as well as to have a good safety stop.

Don't forget to tell the dive operator what your dive plan is!

DIVE 62

DEEP REEF

Diver and sea snake

GPS

N25°04'02.7"
E56°24'25.6"

Depth: 30m | **Snorkelling:** No | **Night dive:** Yes
Distance from harbours: FIMC 4.53nm @ 141°
Distance to other dive sites:
Refinery Reef (p.134) 14.3nm @ 355°
Inchcape 10 (p.124) 3.8nm @ 341°

A deep, but attractive coral plate reef with interesting sea life.

When Scuba International opened their new dive centre from Fujairah Marine Club, they researched the area and, with the help of some of the local fishermen, located this reef in late 2001. They have since buoyed the largest of these coral plates to make locating the reef quick and easy, ensuring that you have the maximum amount of time in which to enjoy this picturesque site.

Diving

Just a 15-20 minute boat ride from Fujairah International Marine Club (FIMC), this deep and flat dive site ranges from 28-30m in depth, depending on the tide. It's an interesting terrain: the area consists primarily of a sandy seabed and several large slab-like plates that dot the contourless sandy bottom and rise up about a metre from the seabed.

Marine Life

As the plate coral rests almost a metre above the seabed it attracts shy marine life: morays who like to hide under the shaded plates and shells keeping themselves out of direct sunlight. If you look closely, you will see shrimp dancing to attract fish to their 'free' cleaning service. It's a very pretty site with various displays of soft corals; green whip or black coral, large branching bottlebrush corals, teddybear corals in various colours and several types of sea fans. It's great to see that all of these corals are in excellent condition due to the strong currents that flow through the area bringing it a rich supply of nutrients. They seem to have lined themselves up, row by row, and where one fan ends, another strategically places itself close by to ensure that every nutritional morsel is absorbed from the water.

Most noticeable here is the abundance of an unusual orange sponge. It's quite unknown from any other site and it looks a bit like spiky chimneys. You will find the usual east coast sea life here: barracuda, turtles, seahorses, snappers, hammour and box fish. Sharp-eyed divers will spot moses sole and rays resting camouflaged on the sandy seabed.

If you are fortunate you may encounter sea snakes here. Admire from a distance as sea snakes are extremely venomous. Instead enjoy watching them poke their heads under the ridge in search of snacks.

Safety

As it's a deep site, you need to take care on this dive and the use of a computer is highly recommended. If you're trained in the use of Nitrox this will help you to maximise your dive time.

NITROX DIVING

Several dive centres offer Nitrox training, (see the Dive Directory on p.184) as does the Desert Sports Diving Club for its members. You can get Nitrox fills and cylinders from Scuba Dubai, DSDC, Scubatec, Sandy Beach Hotel, and Scuba International. Remember to take your N2 diving card with you for proof of certification. Find out more about furthering your dive training on p.150.

Lionfish

DIVE 63

DIBBA ISLAND

Green turtle

GPS

N25°36'14.1"
E56°21'05.9"

Depth: 16m | **Snorkelling:** Yes | **Night dive:** Yes
Distance from harbours:
Dibba Bayah Harbour 5.2nm @ 122°
Khor Fakkan Harbour 15.2nm @ 353°
Lulaya Harbour 12.8nm @ 347°

A site with colourful corals, where you're virtually guaranteed a sighting of a turtle.

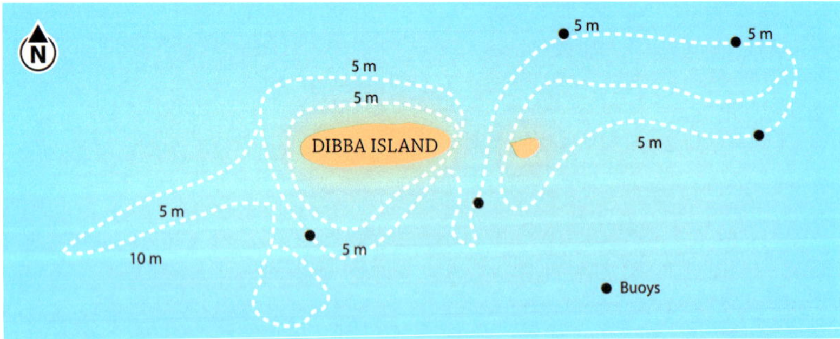

This small rocky island has long sloping sides that are covered by a reef formed by a variety of soft and boulder corals. The side nearest the shore is only 3-4m deep, so it should be dived at high tide. The seaward side has a long sloping rocky reef with many green and purple whip corals that make it a very attractive dive site.

There are two mooring buoys on the site, one located to the north-west end of the island and one to the south east. The buoys are perfectly situated to allow you to dive the seaward side of the site. Just make sure you choose the correct buoy depending on the current!

Diving

If you're in a hurry, it's possible to complete a circuit of the island in one dive, but only at high tide. Regardless of the tide, if you're planning several dives in this area, it's a good idea to explore the wall that runs parallel to the island. The area is prone to both thermoclines and strong currents.

At low tide we recommend you keep to the north (seaward) side of the island, otherwise you'll be snorkelling, instead of diving, on the south (shore) side. At high tide, explore the side of the island that's nearest the mainland. There's a good chance you'll see turtles there.

Dibba Island makes a lovely, easy night dive, and is simple to navigate. There are lots of beautiful, swaying corals that will have their polyps out to feed at night, and you'll find sleeping fish that have lodged themselves between the rocks, often leaving their tails exposed. You may also come across sleeping turtles: do not touch or disturb them as they're easily alarmed. They could actually swallow too much water in their fright and drown. And if you don't disturb them, you'll have more time to examine them close up – a wonderful experience!

Snorkelling

This is one of the best snorkelling sites around, especially for seeing turtles. The turtles are most prolific on the seaward side of the island where there are lots of coral reefs, and it seems that snorkellers are often lucky enough to see turtles, even when divers don't.

Jawfish with eggs

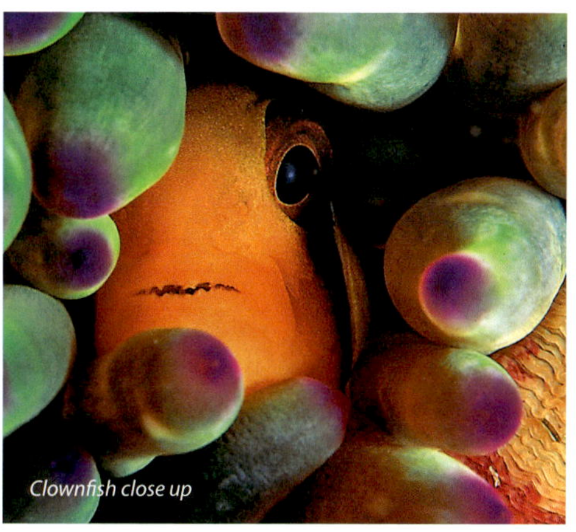

Clownfish close up

Swim to the island if you are a strong swimmer, or go by boat for safety.

Marine Life

You're virtually guaranteed sightings of turtles on this site and you'll see many fish species here too. Look out for the unusual jawfish (or hole goby), noticeable for their rather ugly features – huge heads and large eyes and mouths. They build lovely 'drainpipe' homes, and line the walls with pretty shells to prevent them from collapsing. The drainpipe goes down quite a long way and once the jawfish disappears into it, it takes a long time to reappear. When it's mating season (usually June to August, but it seems to depend on the water temperature), they pop out of their holes, exposing their colourful and beautifully patterned bodies.

Be careful of the resident clownfish – they are sometimes rather aggressive while defending their territory; bashing your mask with some force and giving your fingers a nip!

DIVE 64

HOLE IN THE WALL

Boxfish

GPS
N25°20'26.3"
E56°22'39.7"

Depth: 15m | **Snorkelling:** Yes | **Night dive:** Yes
Distance from harbours: FIMC 4.53nm @ 141°
Distance to other dive sites:
Khor Fakkan Harbour 2.9nm @ 118°

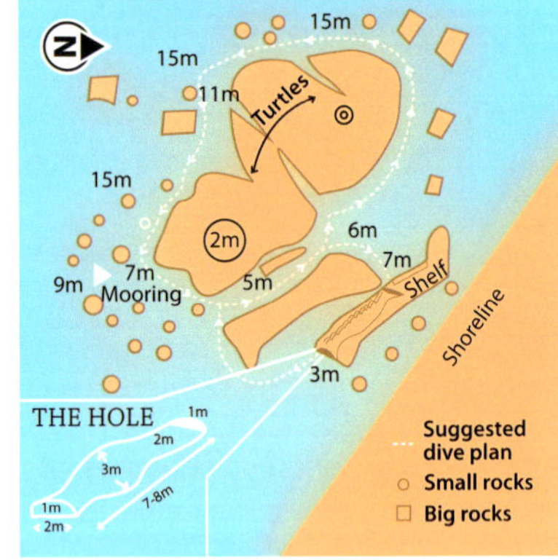

A rocky coral wall that makes a great dive at night, when it's a haven for sleeping fish.

The site is close to where a fuel depot is being constructed and, due to the fact that the mountain behind this area is being levelled to make a harbour, the site still suffers from excessive silt and poor visibility. However, since the completion of the main excavation work, the site does seem to be starting to recover.

Diving

This site consists of a rocky coral outcrop that slopes out to sea. It has a small swim-through that's just large enough for divers to get through comfortably, but considering the visibility on some days, it's not surprising that not everyone finds the 'hole in the wall'!

However, there's a mooring buoy at one end of the submerged rock and if you follow the coral outcrop around to the point where you can swim between it and a second small outcrop, you're on the right track. Continue around the back of the rock until you find yet another outcrop. When you're at about 7m, you should be able to find the hole: it's about 1.5m in diameter at the entrance and it opens up a little more as you swim through it. The

Anemones

WARNING
Before attempting to dive any wreck or cave, or to go through the 'hole in the wall' at this site, it's strongly recommended that you receive adequate training in diving in an overhead environment.

swim-through is about 8m long and varies between 1.5 and 3m in diameter. It's large enough to swim through comfortably, just so long as it's not lined with urchins, and you will see little beams of light coming through a crack in the roof of the rock.

At night this is a haven for sleeping butterflyfish and parrotfish. Only enter if you have good buoyancy control though, or you could end up impaling yourself on the urchins' spikes.

Snorkelling
It's a shallow site and, even if the visibility is poor, snorkellers will enjoy some interesting marine life, particularly if you snorkel close to the wall.

Marine Life
You'll find all the usual east coast underwater creatures here, along with small shrimp enjoying the ride and meals courtesy of some fat pincushion starfish. Look out for purple finger corals beautifully decorated by brittlestars – it looks a bit like the corals are wearing colourful striped scarves. Take the time to peer between all those urchins and see if you can find an elusive needleshrimp, difficult to see because they blend in with the urchin spines. Turtles are regularly seen here, often with remoras clinging on to their shell. Cuttlefish and batfish seem to be prolific for most of the year, and you might find small stingrays in the middle of the swim-through.

Safety
This site is renowned for its sea urchins, so take care with your buoyancy. Also keep an eye out for the bryozoans; they look small, harmless and fern-like, but these tiny creatures deliver a powerful, irritating sting. If there's any surge or waves on the day you're diving, select another site as this is not one to dive in inclement weather.

DIVE 65

INCHCAPE 1

GPS
N25°30'44.8"
E56°22'56.7"

Depth: 32m | **Snorkelling:** No | **Night dive:** Yes
Distance from harbours: FIMC 4.53nm @ 141°
Distance to other dive sites:
Khor Fakkan Harbour 10nm @ 013°
Lulaya Harbour 7.2nm @ 015°

A decommissioned boat that's become home to a wide variety of marine life.

Inchcape 1 – originally known as Gray Swift 2 – was built in the USA by Halter Marine and shipped to Dubai in 1971 or 1972. She started her service in Ras Al Khaimah and in 1991 moved to Dubai where she was renamed Inchcape 1. She was used by Inchcape Shipping Services to transport crew and supplies to and from ships, oil platforms and rigs in both Dubai and Fujairah, and was decommissioned in 2001. General Manager Eric Laing and his colleagues, Captain Joe Finch and Louise Marr of Inchcape Shipping Services decided that the decommissioned boat would be ideal to sink and form an artificial offshore reef.

The engines were removed and cleaned of oil residues, and the doors and hatches were taken off. HRH Sheikh Hamed Bin Mohammed Al Sharqi, Ruler of Fujairah, member of the Supreme Council, granted permission for the boat to be sunk.

Finally, and with the assistance of Dibba Municipality, Sandy Beach Motel, Sandy Beach Dive Centre, Al Boom Marine and Inchcape Shipping Services, the boat was relocated to her final resting place, where she has served as a base for new life.

Snappers

Diving

This is a small vessel that sits upright and faces south. There are car tyres around the gunwales, and remnants of the wheelhouse can be found on the seabed at the stern of the wreck.

The depth of this dive can be more than 30m, depending on the tide. The wreck is small and it's possible to go around it several times during a dive. The best plan is to swim around it slowly, starting from the seabed. After searching for the many residents hiding between the hull and seabed, ascend to the deck area where you can explore the holds and the engine room to see what's hiding.

You will need a light to reveal the colours of the marine life seeking the sanctuary of these dark spaces. The reef on the forward deck is developing rapidly and is home to frog fish, seahorses and some rather large honeycomb moray eels.

The wreck itself is no longer safe to penetrate though, as there are many entanglement hazards.

Wreck register: Not charted
Name: Inchcape 1 originally known as Gray Swift 2
Nationality: United Arab Emirates
Year built: 1971
Type: Steel crew boat
Tonnage: 57 tonnes gross
Dimensions: L: 21m, B: 5m, D: 3m
Cargo: None
Date sunk: December 12, 2001

Whip goby

WARNING

Be aware that with depths of up to 30m, this is a fairly deep site and the currents can be quite strong.

Cardinalfish

Marine Life

From the beginning, fish and a variety of other marine life took up residence on this wreck very rapidly, and they continue to thrive.

If you approach slowly and carefully, you can find large rays hiding under the wreck towards the stern. A large shoal of cardinal fish takes up all the space in the safety of the wheelhouse; they are trying to avoid being eaten by the large barracuda and emperor fish that cruise around outside, waiting for an easy meal.

You will also see large hammour and several species of moray eels hiding in the tyres. Look out for honeycomb morays, pennant fish, boxfish, soldierfish and red bigeyes. The fish life is attracted by the spreading algae. There are more and more fish beginning to congregate on this wreck and you never know what you'll find here!

GOING ARTIFICIAL

The benefit of sinking an old vessel, or even an obsolete rig, is that it provides a habitat for hundreds of underwater species to live and feed on. This is generally a positive change, especially where the seabed is largely flat and featureless. It's no guarantee that a wreck will become a healthy and diverse reef, but the chances are that nature will snap up the opportunity. Turn to A Year In The Life Of Inchcape 2 on p.122 to read an account of a wreck's gradual transformation into a reef.

FISH EYES

Torpedo ray

Parrotfish

Peacock flounder

Broomtailed wrasse

Honeycomb moray

DIVE 66

INCHCAPE 2

Depth: 22m | **Snorkelling:** No | **Night dive:** Yes
Distance from harbours: FIMC 4.53nm @ 141°
Distance to other dive sites:
Khor Fakkan Harbour 1.8nm @ 108°
Lulaya Harbour 3.4nm @ 167°

Practise your wreck penetration skills and explore this rich marine habitat for its treasures.

The boat was built in the USA by Halter Marine and shipped to Dubai on a Hansa Line vessel in 1974, where she started her service before being moved to Fujairah in 1991. She was renamed in 1993 and eventually relocated to Ras Al Khaimah in 1995. She transported crew and supplies to and from ships, oil platforms and rigs during her working life.

Although she had just received a new coat of paint, it was found that she needed considerably more work to make her seaworthy, so the decision was made to decommission her. The artificial reef created when Inchcape 1 was sunk was so successful, and the marine life it attracted in a relatively short time so prolific, that it inspired the Inchcape team, Eric Laing, Captain Joe Finch and Louise Marr to offer Inchcape 2 for the same purposes. This time, the wreck was sunk in shallower waters to make it accessible to the majority of divers.

The boat was moved to Fujairah where she was prepared for her new life underwater. It took more than two weeks to ensure she was clean of oil residues, and the doors and hatches were removed to enable divers to swim through the wreck safely.

Diving

The Inchcape 2 sits listing to her port side in 20-22m with the bow facing 280° degrees. Cyclone Gonu relocated the wreck from her original location and she now sits approximately 40m from the wall between Martini Rock and The Hole in the Wall.

It's possible to enter and swim through the whole wreck, end-to-end, but take care as some of the internal fittings have become loose with age. Entry to the engine room can be gained through the aft deck hatches. Swim through the living quarters, past the bathroom and when you've seen enough, you can exit via the stairs at either side of the wreck. If you're more adventurous and of medium build, you can exit through the bow hatchway. Take care if you choose this route; while it's quite easy and safe, you need to ensure that your equipment doesn't get snagged.

Inchcape 2's deck

Divers looking into the wheelhouse

The best way to enjoy this wreck is to go down the buoy line, currently connected to the starboard side of the stern. Move slowly around the vessel and explore the seabed; you'll probably find some large jawfish hiding in the debris. You may be able to make out the ship's name on the stern, although it is now encrusted with calcareous worms and various algae and bryozoans.

Once you've made your way around the wreck, ascend to the deck area through

Wreck register: Not charted
Name: Inchcape 2, originally known as Gray Lance
Nationality: United Arab Emirates
Year built: 1971
Type: Steel crew boat
Tonnage: 57 tonnes gross
Dimensions: L: 21m, B: 5m, D: 3m
Cargo: None
Date sunk: April 24, 2002

the engine room and swim along to the bow. Alternatively, you can look in from the outside. Shine your torch inside the engine room and you'll find lots of juvenile fish of many breeds hiding between the engine parts and pipes. The wheelhouse is spacious and you can easily enter and exit through the gaping holes.

Marine Life

The wreck is located between Martini Rock (p.128) and Hole in the Wall (p.112). The abundant fish life of these two sites has spread quickly to occupy this new habitat. Already there are rays, moray eels, juvenile barracuda, jacks and cardinals benefiting from this new wreck.

During the initial months of its underwater incarnation, the wreck was covered with small white anemones, that carpeted the decks and railings, giving it a ghostly glow, and jewelled anemones.

Plumbline

Various sponges, young teddybear corals, encrusting worms and algae have also rapidly taken over the wreck and are enjoying their new home. There have been some sightings of frogfish and seahorses, and nudibranchs are a big highlight.

WHAT'S THE WEATHER LIKE?

Dive centres will check the weather conditions before they venture out. If you want to find out for yourself before diving, then either check with a dive centre, or try these apps: Windguru (give wind speeds and gusts by the hour), Windalert and TidesPlanner.

Jewel anemones

Decorator crab on teddybear coral

Teddybear coral

Feather star

A YEAR IN THE LIFE OF INCHCAPE 2

An artificial reef sounds like a contradiction in terms. But when manmade objects are cleaned of their residues and toxins, and deliberately sunk, marine life is often quick to take up residence. This is an account of how the sea and its inhabitants came to call Inchcape 2 home.

Within the first two months of Inchcape 2 being sunk on 24 April 2002, the first marine organisms began to make an appearance. Small limpets and barnacles started to take hold of all the surfaces, and were followed shortly by small algae and seaweed growths. Next came the calcareous tube worms that made pretty patterns all over the ship's blue paintwork.

This activity and growth increased over the next two months and suddenly it seemed as though the wreck had developed a thick carpet of algae, anemones and tusk-shaped worm tubes.

The fourth month also saw small teddybear corals starting to take shape like little snowballs scattered over the deck. By the fifth month, the fish world had discovered the wreck. Fish, invariably snappers and batfish, started to gather in large shoals – in fact, you sometimes couldn't find the wreck for the fish! The teddybear corals, sponges and algae had grown considerably by this time too.

From the seventh month onwards, an even more varied amount of marine life was found. Small blennies took up residence in some of the pipes and small cowry shells camouflaged themselves on the teddybear corals. Around about this time, nudibranchs made an appearance, possibly attracted by the algae and bryozoans that were growing well at this stage. Some strange spaghetti-like algae also appeared.

This continued into the eighth month. The sponges were growing well and small gobies began to take up residence inside them. By now, the wreck was covered in feather stars and for several months there was the strange phenomenon of clouds of non-stinging jellyfish that hung around the site.

Three frogfish appeared on the wreck in its ninth month as an underwater habitat. These must have been the most photographed frogfish in the world as for most divers in the UAE this was their first opportunity to see a frogfish up close. They hung around for a few months and then disappeared. They haven't been seen since.

The wreck continued to flourish with 'mushroom' jellyfish flying like UFOs over the site, and numerous varieties of crabs, crayfish, squat lobsters and decorator crabs becoming regular sightings. Divers can count on it being encapsulated by shoals of snappers.

Coming up to the anniversary of the wreck sinking, it was now entirely covered with some sort of growth; algae, teddybear corals, whip corals and hydrozoans, all of which was inhabited by crabs, lobsters, shells and nudibranchs.

Diving on the Inchcape 2, whatever the season, always provides something interesting and different for the photographer and diver.

UNDERWATER PHOTOGRAPHY

A site like Inchcape 2, with its many tiny marine creatures, is just the kind of dive that's likely to spark off an interest in underwater photogra otography, which is often the route that most people follow when embarking on this new passion. And with digital cameras and underwater housings, photography is an aspect of diving that is rapidly becoming more accessible to people.

Underwater photography is not simply photography that takes place under the surface of the sea, though. Even professional photographers find themselves struggling to adapt to conditions underwater. There's the water to contend with for starters: water refracts light, is full of little particles that show up as a snowstorm on your pictures, and it absorbs colour. To counter the effects, you need to get as close as possible to your subject, and you'll need to learn how to use flashes (called strobes). Getting up close to that nudibranch also requires excellent buoyancy control – it's no use photographing the reef's rich marine life if you're bumping into it and destroying it as you go along. It's also a tricky thing learning to master your equipment, let alone diving with it. Using it and setting up a shot while maintaining your buoyancy becomes an art in its own right.

That said, with a little practice and the aid of the many underwater photography courses that are on offer today, this could be your next big thing – turn to p.154 for more information on how to get started and what sort of equipment you will need. The sense of accomplishment when you get that perfectly framed shot is addictive and you'll keep coming back for more.

DIVE 67

INCHCAPE 10

GPS
N25°07'36.1"
E56°23'05.3"

Depth: 24m | **Snorkelling:** No | **Night dive:** Yes
Distance from harbours:
FIMC 1.53nm @ 090°

An always-varied and interesting site for trained wreck divers.

This is the third ship Inchcape Shipping Services (ISS) has sunk to form an artificial reef (see p.114 and p.118). As ISS is a Fujairah based company, special permission was sought from the authorities and HH Sheikh Hamad bin Mohammed Al Sharqi, Ruler of Fujairah, member of the Supreme Council, gave his approval for the project.

The boat, originally named Jetwise, was built in Singapore in 1982 and was initially owned by a company in Bahrain. ISS bought her in 1998 and she was moved to Fujairah where she transported crew and supplies to and from ships and oil rigs. What makes her unusual is that she was propelled by three water jets.

As with the other Inchcape wrecks, ISS spent a considerable amount of time and money ensuring the boat was environmentally friendly and equipped for her new life underwater. On the whole, the Inchcape wrecks are considered a success as they've attracted an incredible amount of marine life within a relatively short period of time, and they've taken the burden off some of the other dive sites.

Diving

This is the largest of the Inchcapes and she sits upright at 24m with the bow facing north. You should consider penetrating the vessel only if you are a trained wreck diver. If so, you can enter from the engine room at the back and swim through the living quarters and up one of the sets of stairs.

The best way to enjoy this site is to go down the buoy, connected to the starboard side of the stern, slowly work your way around the wreck and explore the seabed where you may find some rays resting. Once you've gone around it, enter the wreck (with the above caution in mind) and ascend to the deck area through the engine room. Alternatively, you can swim around the deck perimeter and shine your torch inside the engine room, wheelhouse and crew quarters to spot the many varieties of juvenile fish that stick closely together in small shoals.

The wheelhouse is easily entered and exited and while you're there, you should take a look at the ship's horns on the wheelhouse roof which always seem to stay reasonably shiny and algae-free. You can then move up to the upper deck area where you can play with the controls. Swim over to the mooring rope for a nice slow ascent, remembering to complete a safety stop.

This is an easy site to get to for a night dive, thanks to its proximity to the harbour. But take care if you've already completed a dive or two during the day as your bottom time may be limited. It's quite an eerie night dive, but you'll see creatures that you don't normally spot in the daylight like morays, crabs and shrimps.

Wreck register: Not charted
Name: Jetwise
Nationality: United Arab Emirates
Year built: 1982
Type: Steel crew boat
Tonnage: 84 tonnes gross
Dimensions: L: 27m, B: 6m, D: 4m
Cargo: None
Date sunk: June 28, 2003

Blenny

Marine Life

Since this wreck was purposely located close to another artificial reef, the fish have homed in on it. In its first few months it acted as a nursery and you could find most species of fish in miniature on it; banner fish, hammour, lionfish, snappers, jacks, filefish, morays and a juvenile snake. It became covered in a layer of hairy, dark red and brown algae and some small calcerated worms began to encrust the surface areas, particularly on the windows and other glass bits. Now, a few years down the line, the marine life on it is constantly changing and every dive holds another interesting discovery.

Safety

You need to use dive tables or a computer on this dive; it's a square profile and time is limited. Make sure that you descend and ascend the buoy rope and always complete a safety stop. As with all wrecks, watch out for sharp edges that might cut or snag you.

DIVE 68

INES

GPS

N 25°11'21.8"
E56°27'30.6"

Depth: 72m | **Snorkelling:** No | **Night dive:** No
Distance from harbours:
FIMC 6.2nm. @ 062°

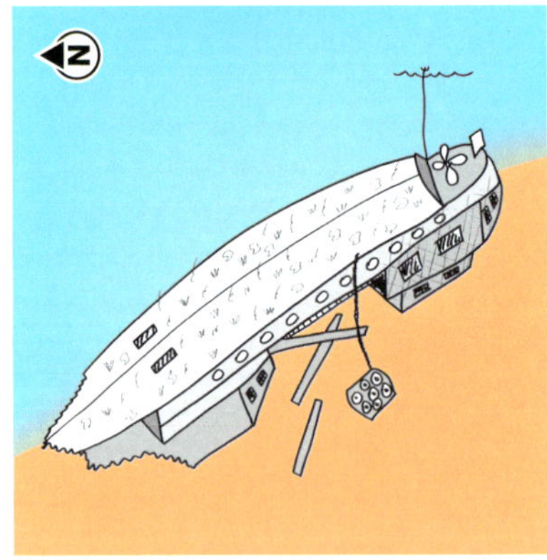

A deep, technical dive that makes a good entry-level option for Trimix divers.

While the Ines was anchored about 13km off Fujairah in August 1999, there was an explosion on board that resulted in a fire. Five crew members were reported missing, two were injured, 22 rescued and there was one fatality.

Diving

The DSDC Dive Club has buoyed the wreck with a buoy 1.5m under the surface, which is attached at the other end near the propeller. There appears to be a thermocline anywhere between nine and 30m on each and every dive made on this wreck. The thermocline temperature can change by up to 5°C and can create a thick sludge of bad visibility. Once you're underneath the thermocline though, the visibility is usually very good.

As you reach the bottom of the anchor rope you will be at a depth of 55m. This is where the propellers are, as the wreck is completely upside down. You can then proceed to the seabed at 70-72m and start to work your way around the wreck.

As she lies upside down, the structure of the ship has been destroyed but there are one or two areas where you can go underneath her and come out the other side. You can see some portholes amidships towards the stern and some railings are visible. On the ship's starboard side you'll find a large sunken mooring buoy full of tyres.

It is possible to go inside the wreck down the corridor, however, it's imperative that you're aware of your surroundings and bottom time at all times. The bow is damaged and it appears that this is where most of the explosion and fire damage happened. You can then work your way from 70m back to the prop at 55m by swimming up the hull, which is sprinkled with soft and hard coral growths, and you will notice some anodes still visible even though the wreck's been down there for a relatively short time. Then start your long, slow ascent making the necessary decompression and safety stops using the relevant air mixes.

Marine Life

This wreck is not dived as often as other dive sites, due to its depth, and the fish life varies according to the time of the year you visit it. Still, you're likely to encounter several fish, including: jacks, tuna, rays, guitar sharks, hammour, cutlass fish, barracuda and cuttlefish.

FOR TECHNICAL DIVERS ONLY

This dive is not for sport divers as it's considered too deep for compressed air diving. Ines lies at 70m+ and it's imperative that you're trained to dive at this depth as it's outside what is considered safe for sport divers. Ines is however, a good entry level dive for Trimix diving (see the write-up on technical diving in Further Info). All divers should be familiar with decompression diving with a Nitrox mix for decompression and able to deploy an SMB from blue water in an emergency. With this type of diving it is also imperative to have various safety measures – safety divers, oxygen cylinders and so forth – on board.

Wreck register: Unknown
Name: Ines
Nationality: Belize
Year built: April 1967
Type: Oil barge/tanker
Tonnage: 6174 DWT
Dimensions: L: 112m, B: 15.8m, D: 6.9m
Cargo: None
Date sunk: 9 August 1999

DIVE 69

MARTINI ROCK

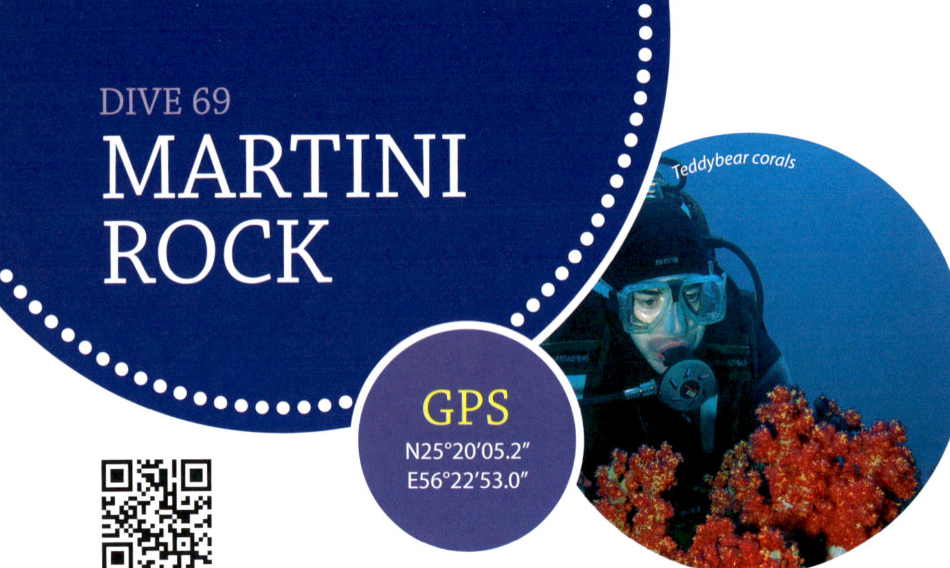
Teddybear corals

GPS
N25°20'05.2"
E56°22'53.0"

Depth: 3-22m | **Snorkelling:** Yes | **Night dive:** Yes
Distance from harbours:
Khor Fakkan Harbour 2nm @ 122°
Lulaya Harbour 3.6nm @ 179°

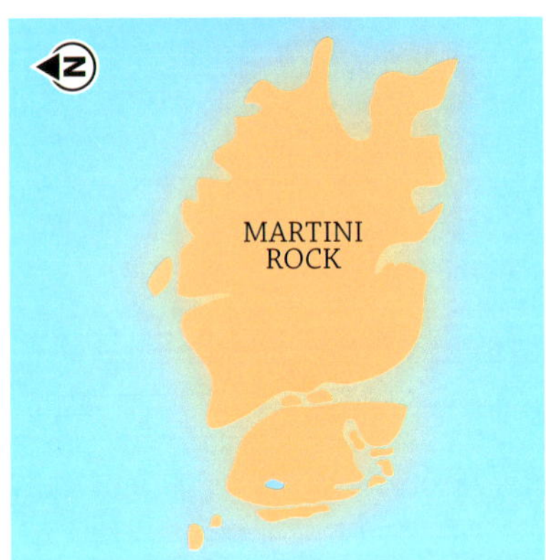

A pleasing and colourful site that makes you feel like you're diving in an aquarium

Martini Rock is a small, submerged coral outcrop, the top of which is visible from the surface at 3m. The rock has several sandy gullies or alleys and most of it is covered in orange and purple teddybear coral, which makes for a pleasing and colourful dive site. This is an excellent site for divers of all skill levels, and a favourite east coast location.

Diving

The north side of the rock is the deepest, going down to 22m, while the rest of the site is at about 13m. There's enough time to complete a circuit of the rock in one dive, but note that the site is prone to both thermoclines and strong currents at times.

The variety of fish life is excellent and the top 5m is like an aquarium – schools of snapper, fusiliers, anthias, red tooth triggerfish and large-mouth mackerel are present for most of the year.

Martini Rock is an excellent option for a night dive, although if you don't know the site well, navigation may be a problem. You may see sleeping turtles, rays out feeding and perhaps a spotted eagle ray.

Hawkfish

At night the rock appears completely red because of all the feeding teddybear corals. Look closely into the soft corals to find fish, such as juvenile damselfish or hawkfish, that use the coral as a safe haven from the larger hunters that are out looking for dinner. If you stay near the bottom of the rock on the seabed, you may see large rays sifting through the sand in search of small molluscs and crustaceans. They will come right up to you at night and can cause quite a scare!

You may also encounter large pufferfish that swim about at night oblivious of their surroundings, bumping around rather as if they were in a pinball machine! Don't shine your torch at them for too long, as they'll become completely disorientated.

At night you could come across a strange looking fish called a long finned waspfish (a type of gurnard). They appear to run over the seabed on three spider-like legs, that are hidden underneath their winged fins. They have two pronged feelers extending from their mouths that they use to search for creatures hidden in the silty seabed.

Snorkelling

For snorkellers, this is a great, rocky, shallow location that teems with life. The top of the rock is about 2-3m from the surface (depending on the tide), and the bright colours of the teddybear corals decorating the rock are easily seen. You may also see boxfish, jacks and many shoals of fish near the surface. If you can duck dive down to 5m or more, you may see morays, rays and perhaps a turtle.

Marine Life

Large sections of the rock are covered in red, purple and orange teddybear corals, with one side swathed in purple whip corals, and green and yellow whip corals in a deep corner. There are also clumps of featherstars that hide shrimps, Omani clingfish and nudibranchs.

WARNING

During their mating season (June to August), the red tooth triggerfish found on this site become territorial – darting towards you, only to turn away at the last moment. A triggerfish's territory extends upwards in a cone shape, so to get out of their territory always swim horizontally away from them, rather than up.

Hammour over coral reef

DIVE 70

MURBAH REEF

Yellow-mouth moray

GPS

N25°16'21.0"
E56°22'31.6"

Depth: 5-14m | **Snorkelling:** Yes | **Night dive:** Yes

Distance from harbours:
FIMC 14.3nm @ 006°
Khor Fakkan Harbour 8.2nm. @ 171°
Lulaya Harbour 8.4nm. @ 175°

Distance from other dive sites:
Ras Qidfa (p.132) 3.1nm @ 187°
Refinery Reef (p.134) 1.1nm @ 196°

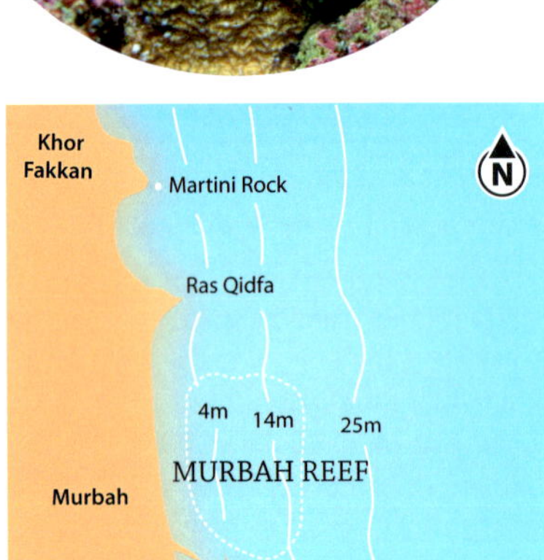

A shallow reef full of vivid corals and curious fish.

This is another site discovered by Scuba International, this one in the summer of 2001. What sets Murbah Reef apart is that it's covered with hard corals all competing for space – in fact, it's difficult to see the seabed thanks to the dense coral growth.

Diving

The reef stretches for about 400m along the coastline. At 5-14m it's ideal for the last dive of the day or for beginners with excellent buoyancy control. If you're diving the site at night, we recommend that you arrive at the reef just prior to sunset so that you can anchor in a sandy patch and wait for darkness. The site is quite noisy at night, thanks to all the corals that become active after dark. You'll see various shrimps, crabs and morays, and possibly even a sleeping turtle.

Snorkelling

The site is very attractive and shallow enough for snorkellers even when visibility isn't great. It's an excellent spot to find small fish hiding in the corals, and it's also good to see so many healthy hard corals thriving at this shallow depth, especially when you consider the wide range of water temperatures here.

Marine Life

The attraction of this reef is the large number of hard corals, primarily staghorn but also brain and uncommon cauliflower corals. As it's a shallow reef, you can see the coral polyps' unusual colourations of pinks, purples and blues.

The reef is also home to numerous fish. Clownfish in their anemone hosts, and plenty of morays which are really quite shy despite their fierce looks and those nasty teeth (which point backwards to prevent any morsels from escaping!). The reef teems with Picasso triggerfish, with their cream-coloured bodies streaked with orange and blue and a large black stripe through the eye area. They have small, toothy mouths and you will find them hunting and feeding on shrimps and sea urchins using their strong teeth.

Staghorn corals

The fish on this reef don't appear to receive too many visitors, and as a result some are very inquisitive and seem happy to pose for a few photos before dashing back into the corals.

WARNING

When you go snorkelling, you need to keep your skin protected from the sun – because you're in the water you often don't realise you're burning until it's way too late. Wearing a T-shirt isn't enough: it will leave the backs of your legs exposed and sunburn behind your knees is particularly painful. You can wear a 0.5mm wetsuit or a shortie, or at the very least a rash vest. Whatever you choose, make sure you supplement it with plenty of sunblock, especially on your neck and ears.

DIVE 71

RAS QIDFA

Slipper lobster

GPS
N25°19'27.2"
E56°22'56.0"

Depth: 8m | **Snorkelling:** Yes | **Night dive:** Yes
Distance from harbours:
Khor Fakkan Harbour 2.7nm @ 150°
Lulaya Harbour 4.3nm @ 164°

A small and rocky headland that's full of hard corals and tiny, interesting critters.

Leading into the bay towards Martini Rock, Ras Qidfa is a small, rocky headland where you'll find many hard corals and rocky boulders to explore.

Diving

It's best to start your dive at the southern end of Ras Qidfa, and travel north towards Martini Rock bay, keeping the rocks, boulders and wall on your left-hand side. There's plenty to see here, including a multitude of fish species, turtles and hard and soft corals, although it becomes a little less interesting if you leave the rocky shores and venture onto the sandy seabed.

At night, simply follow the wall, keeping it on your left, and look in the nooks and crannies in the rocks for banded shrimp, slipper lobsters and crayfish – it's an easy and pleasant spot for a dive after dark. There are not as many corals here as there are on other sites in the area, but you may be rewarded with glimpses of sleeping turtles, rays or even spotted eagle rays.

Snorkelling

This is a good spot for snorkellers, especially if you enjoy the marine life on the seabed. It's a shallow site, and you will see most of the fish by staying close to the shoreline. If you venture further out you're probably only going to see moses sole but, then again, you might also be rewarded with the sight of rays or turtles.

Marine Life

There's plenty of fish life to see here; regularly spotted species include fusiliers, jacks and triggerfish. Look out for turtles and crayfish too.

If you search the featherstars carefully, you might find small shrimps and squat lobsters in them. These little critters camouflage themselves by changing their colours to match those of their hosts. There are also soft and hard corals that put on a show at night when they feed.

Squat lobster

Hard coral

Courting nudibranchs

DIVE 72

REFINERY REEF

Porcelain squat lobster and shrimps

GPS
N25°18'22.7"
E56°23'10.9"

Depth: 28m | **Snorkelling:** No | **Night dive:** Yes
Distance from harbours:
FIMC 10.8nm. @ 008°

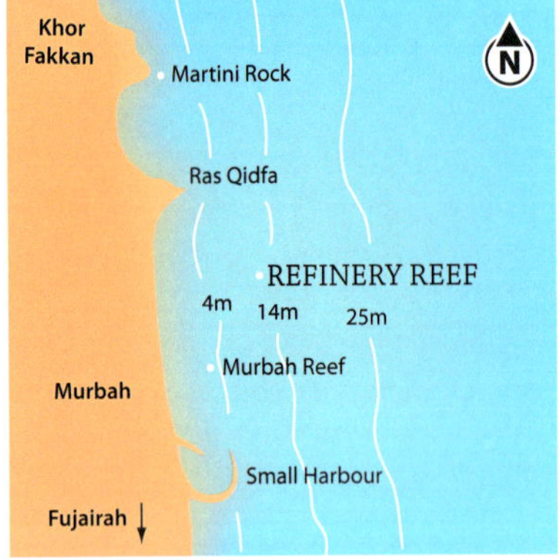

An expansive coral site where you might spot some odd fish antics.

This is another reef located by Scuba International and it's very similar to Deep Reef (p.108) in that the site consists of a sandy seabed with several slabs of plate corals, and other coral outcrops.

Diving

Going by boat, Refinery Reef is about 25 minutes or so from the Fujairah International Marine Club. It lies between 24 and 28m which means it's not a site for snorkellers. For divers though it offers a chance to see some varied corals and some interesting marine life.

Marine Life

This area is quite spread out, rather similar to Anemone and Coral Gardens in Khor Fakkan, and boasts all the usual types of corals – green whip corals and teddybear corals in shades of pink, orange and red. There's also plenty of an unusual pretty yellow soft coral called solenocaulon. Solenocaulon is covered with polyps on one side, and flat on the other.

If you approach slowly and look carefully, you can sometimes find small yellow gobies and squat lobsters hiding on the same coral. The lobsters will defend their

Lionfish

territory from you by holding up their long claws. You may also find a large and rather ugly flat fish called a turbot here. It looks very aggressive with its unusual eyes and many pointed teeth. If you get too close it will give you a start with the speed at which it swims out of your way.

Don't take the aggression too lightly: we were recently trying to photograph one on the seabed. As it didn't seem too phased by us, we tried to get closer for a picture of its amazing eyes. It began to swim away then appeared to have a change of heart and rapidly swam back and bit a diver on the arm. Luckily we were wearing wetsuits as it was winter and the diver got off with a few holes in the wetsuit and a bruised arm (and ego)!

Another unusual aspect of this site is the number of red tooth blue triggerfish that congregate here. During mating season, which is usually between June and August, these fish are fiercely territorial. If you attract their attention and they see you as a threat they'll charge at you, turning away only at the very last moment and just avoiding contact. Wearing blue fins seems to attract even more unwelcome attention from them. So time your dives so as not to coincide with summer if possible.

There's a jellyfish 'season' twice a year, usually from March to April and October to November. If you're diving here then take a close look as the jellyfish act as flying saucers, carrying all sorts of 'aliens' along in the current. Try and spot the juvenile fish, crabs and shrimps hiding in their tentacles – but be careful as most jellies have a nasty sting!

Red-toothed triggerfish

DIVE 73

SHARK ISLAND

GPS
N25°21'12.0"
E56°22'36.2"

Depth: 16m | **Snorkelling:** Yes | **Night dive:** Yes
Other names: Khor Fakkan Island
Distance from harbours:
Khor Fakkan Harbour 0.8nm @ 081°
Lulaya Harbour 2.5nm @ 183°
Distance from other dive sites:
Anemone Gardens (p.102) 0.2nm @ 318°
Coral Gardens (p.106) 0.18nm @ 270°

A great spot for chilling on the beach, diving, snorkelling and, yes, spotting a shark.

This fairly large island stands proud at the south-eastern end of the magnificent Khor Fakkan bay. It has a great beach for picnicking on, to dive and snorkel from, or simply to spend a relaxing day in the sun.

Diving

The depth around the island varies: from a shallow 3-5m on the coastal side, it becomes deeper towards the seaward side. The bottom is sandy and rocky, with a variety of hard and soft corals. The island can be dived from its beach, but most divers are dropped off at either Coral Gardens or Anemone Gardens, and complete the latter part of the dive close to the island. Diving or swimming around the whole island is too far to travel during one dive.

On the south-west tip of the island is a site known as Shark Drift. This is best dived by starting at the deeper seaward-most point at 16m. Drift with the slight current and head around the island. This is an excellent and easy site to dive at night. There's usually lots of fish life to be found, including sleeping turtles in the rocky overhangs. You may also find large, tailless rays. These inquisitive creatures are wonderfully graceful, and look a bit like flying saucers from outer space. They're also often covered in several remoras that attach themselves with the sucker-disc on their head.

Be careful of discarded fishing nets, especially at night. If you do get tangled up in one, don't panic; stay still and signal to your buddy for help. The island is also covered with black urchins, that become active at night, so watch your buoyancy to avoid painful punctures!

Snorkelling

The snorkelling is sometimes better than the diving here, and the waters are shallow enough to be able to see the seabed from the surface. If you want to see sharks, stay at the south-western corner of the island.

During the winter months you're more likely to see blacktip reef sharks swimming in the shallow waters at 1-3m. You'll also find lots of hard and soft corals, turtles and rays if the visibility is good.

Pufferfish

Blacktip shark

Marine Life

As the name suggests, this is a good place for sharks; particularly blacktip reef sharks that can be seen between November and April on the eastern point of the island.

On the seabed you may see cerianthid anemones, pretty purple or white fronds sticking out of a cardboard looking tube. Don't disturb or touch them as they'll retract down into their tubes.

This area is also the haunt of many schools of fish, from batfish and juvenile barracuda to big mouth mackerel, as well as cute pufferfish, large rays with remoras following them, and the occasional spotted eagle ray in shallower water. During the winter months, you may sometimes see murex shells laying their straw-like eggs under the rocks.

WARNING

The rocks around the island are covered with sea urchins and, at certain times of the year, with small brown swimming anemones that deliver a nasty sting if touched (see First Aid, in Further Info for more information).

DIVE 74

SHARM ROCKS

GPS
N25°28'55.0"
E56°21'57.1"

Depth: 14m | **Snorkelling:** Yes | **Night dive:** Yes
Other names: Three Rocks, Pinnacles, Rock Piles
Distance from harbours:
Khor Fakkan Harbour 8.7nm @ 353°
Lulaya Harbour 5.3nm @ 348°

Rich in marine life, this is a great site for leisurely sightseeing, particularly at night.

Not far from Snoopy Island and the Sandy Beach Motel are these four small outcrops of rock that just break the surface of the water at low tide. They are covered in masses of soft corals and there is a small table coral reef towards the shore in about 4m of water.

Note that navigation can be difficult here as the small sandy gullies or alleys leading between the rocks can be misleading and disorientating.

A single mooring buoy can be found on the north side of the rocks sitting in around 8m of water; it is advised to use the mooring as throwing an anchor can cause significant damage to the large reef extending from the site.

Diving

It is possible to complete a circuit of these rocks in one dive, but it can be a rush, even in 60 minutes. The seaward side of the rocks consists of a vertical rocky wall that goes down to 14m, while the shore side has a shallow table coral reef to one side and boulder coral outcrops on the other. This is another excellent shallow site for night dives, but take your time, as it's

Coral crab

crammed with marine life. Peer into the corals for fish seeking protection from the night hunters. You will find lots of sleeping parrotfish, broomtailed wrasse, barracuda and sometimes sleeping turtles. Recently black tipped reef sharks have started to populate the site and can be found in the shallows at the western end of the site.

If you look hard, you may find what appears to be a piece of moving coral strolling around the seabed. It's actually attached to a sandy, dusty looking crab. This is a decorator crab and there are many different species here. The crab steals pieces of coral polyps from the main coral colony and attaches them to its own body for camouflage – incredible!

Snorkelling

The variety of fish life makes Sharm Rocks a very special location for snorkellers, and for some reason the parrotfish, boxfish and broomtailed wrasse appear to be larger here than elsewhere. All these fish are visible when snorkelling and you may also see rays and turtles. On one dive we did, the snorkellers, who were above us, even saw a large barracuda that we failed to see from down below!

If you're a strong swimmer, you can swim out to the rocks from the mainland in about 10 minutes (depending on the weather), but hire a boat if you tire easily.

Marine Life

These rocks are full of shoals of fish; jacks, big mouth mackerel, fusiliers and sometimes squid. You may also see turtles, morays, crayfish and guitar sharks. Explore the bottom for moses soles – their mottled scales provide excellent camouflage against the seabed. All that gives them away is the tiny gold flecks on their bodies. In early evening at the beginning of the warmer months, you can see the strange and beautiful mating habits of boxfish and cuttlefish. At the same time, look out for the small, but fierce, clownfish defending their anemone host, which hides and protects their brood of eggs. Clown fish look cute, but resist the temptation to touch them.

Juvenile lionfish

DIVE 75

SNOOPY ISLAND

Depth: 8m | **Snorkelling:** Yes | **Night dive:** Yes
Other names: Jazirat Al Gubbah
Distance from harbours:
Khor Fakkan Harbour 8nm @ 359°
Lulaya Harbour 5.5nm @ 350°

Marine life on your doorstep! It doesn't get much more accessible than this.

Named because it's shaped like Snoopy lying on his back with his nose in the air (if you've a vivid imagination), the slopes of this small island are covered by several varieties of hard coral that are home to a wealth of anemones and clownfish.

At high tide, it's a good 10 minute swim to the edge of the island. However, during November there are unusually high and low tides that make it possible to walk to the island without getting wet!

Snoopy Island can be visited from Sandy Beach Motel, which has a dive operator whose facilities you can use and where you can hire equipment. If you don't hire equipment and have non-divers with you, there is a beach entrance fee of around Dhs.100. The site is also accessible from the public beach slightly north of the motel.

In an attempt to protect its guests, the motel prohibits anyone from using boats and jet skis around the island. However, boats still occasionally pass between the island and the shore, so take care.

Diving

Snoopy Island is the only shore dive on the east coast, making it one of the easiest

Yellow-mouth moray eel

(and most affordable) dives, seeing as you don't have to rely on a dive operator.

The southern side of the island offers the more interesting diving. There's plenty to see here, including varied and plentiful marine life and several species of hard and soft corals and anemones.

On a night dive, the trip from the shore to the island is very interesting; look out for sleeping fish, as well as starfish, sand dollars, crabs and molluscs, all busy looking for their evening meal. You'll also see shrimps, but only because their eyes shine out from the sand. Try turning your torch off for a moment and seeing how many you can spot.

When you arrive at the rocks and corals at the base of the island, we suggest you turn right, keeping the island on your left. You'll encounter sleeping fish, morays and the occasional barracuda. There are also a few anemones with sleeping clownfish. Sometimes the anemones completely close up, resembling a big, blue plastic bag. We were almost chased out of the water by a lionfish on a night dive here when we persisted in taking too many photos of it. The resident turtles are also a regular sighting.

Snorkelling

Snoopy Island is the most accessible east coast location for snorkellers and is relatively protected from all weather, except exceptionally heavy seas. The site is popular and, on weekends, can be rather busy. But it's also a very shallow site, so you'll be able to see plenty of marine life. Snorkellers are often more likely than divers to encounter guitar and blacktip sharks that appear in the cooler months.

Marine Life

There's a lot of marine life to see, although there's less coral on the shore side than on the seaward side. You can expect to see big mouth mackerel, morays, anemones, clownfish and lionfish. You may also see turtles and sharks. Look out for smaller marine life such as pipefish, shrimps, crabs, and nudibranchs, too.

Tiger shrimp

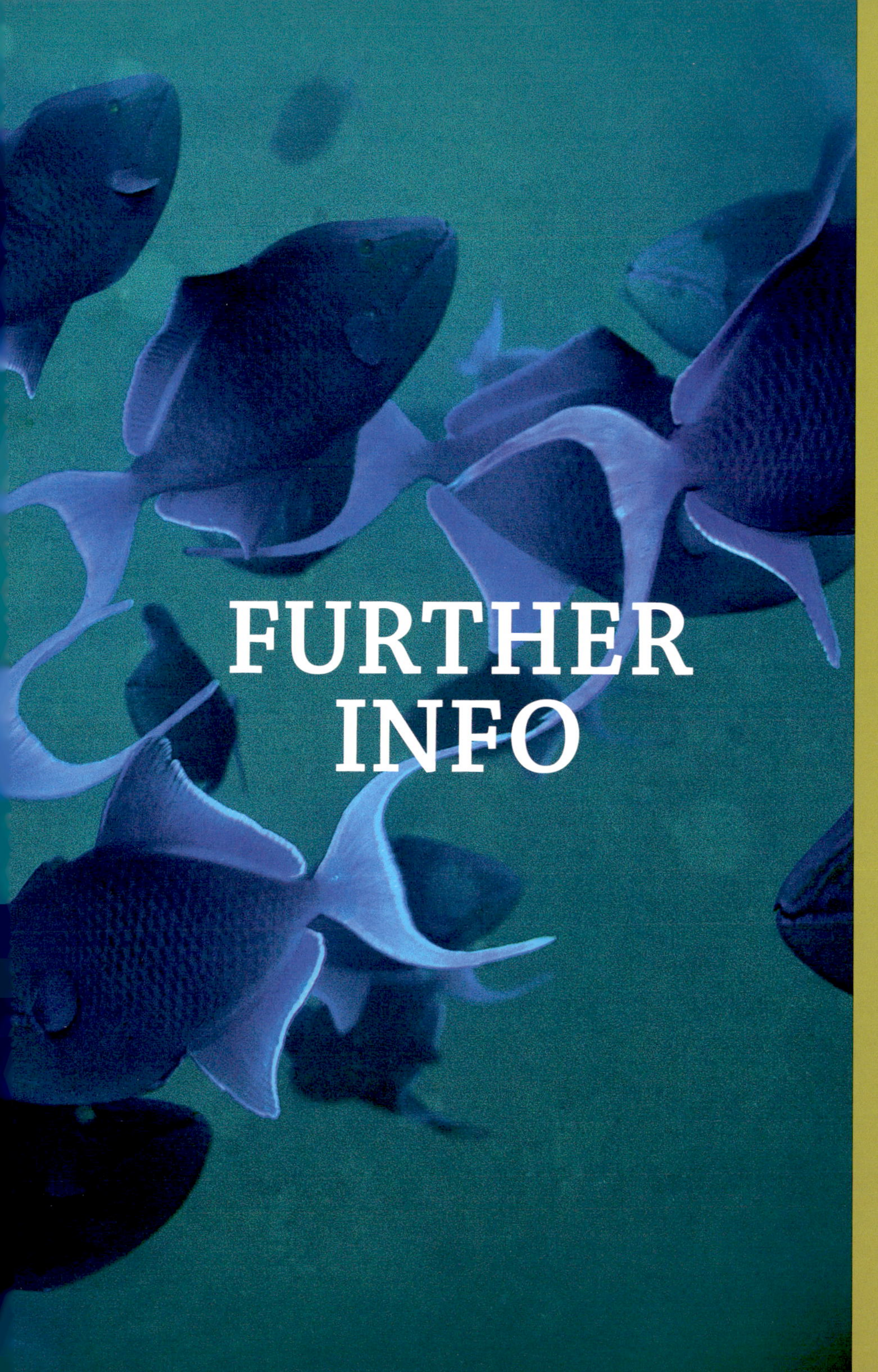

FURTHER INFO

NATURAL WORLD

Marine life in the region's waters is varied. Here are some of the creatures you can hope to see.

Marine Life

The shallow warm waters here allow for reefs that teem with fish, while dugongs graze on sea grass beds and turtles come ashore to lay their eggs. For more information on the region's marine life, check out the books listed in the Bibliography.

Clownfish

Amphiprion ocellaris

Several species of this fish are common residents of coral reefs, where they live among the arms of the sea anemone. While the sea anemone's sting kills other fish, the clownfish is immune to the poison and feeds on the host's leftovers.

Bottlenose Dolphin

Tursiops truncatus

This is the largest of the eight species of dolphin that have been recorded in UAE waters. They are often encountered on east coast boat trips, when they come to play around the boat and show off their amazing acrobatic skills. Other dolphins that live here are the common, the spinner and the humpback dolphin. Whales are also represented in this region by four species of toothed whales, as well as the enormous sperm whale.

Blacktip Reef Shark

Carcharhinus melanopterus

There are at least 10 species of sharks in UAE waters, including reef, blacktip, hammerheads and tiger sharks. Very few of the potentially dangerous sharks come in close enough to shore to present a problem to swimmers. The pearl divers of old considered themselves to be more at risk from barracuda attacks.

Paper Nautilus

Argonauta hians

This extraordinary shell can be found on the beaches of the Arabian Gulf during February and March. The beautiful, feather-light structure is made by the argonaut octopus and held underneath her belly

after she's deposited her eggs in it. Baby octopuses have a protected environment until the mother lets them go and their cradle washes up on the beach.

Sundial Shell

Architectonica perspectiva

The east coast beaches have different shells to those of the Arabian Gulf coast. The sundial shell can be found on Kalba beach, while further north is a good place to find the opercula (plate-like structures that close the opening of a shell when the organism is retracted) of a sea snail.

Manta Ray

Manta birostris

Like sharks, rays are cartilaginous fish, which means that their skeleton is made of a tough, elastic substance rather than bone. There are many different kinds of rays – manta, eagle, bull and marble rays are just a few types seen off the Gulf coast.

Most rays feed on crustaceans, molluscs and oysters, and are bottom dwellers. Some, like the manta ray, prefer open water and feed on plankton.

While the stingray does inflict an excruciatingly painful sting, all the other rays are harmless and none are aggressive. The stingray prefers to hide and tends to bury itself in sand in shallow water and may be inadvertently stepped on by bathers, so shuffle your feet to scare them off.

Sea Cow or Dugong

Dugong dugon

This is the animal that gave rise to the legend of the mermaid, though it's highly unlikely that you will ever see it. Related to elephants and rock hyrax, it has breasts between its front legs, nails instead of claws, and lives in herds led by a female. There are probably less than a thousand of these gentle creatures left in the Gulf, where they face the continual hazards of shipping, oil pollution and degradation of the sea grasses that they feed on. The Arabic name 'arus al bahr' means 'bride of the sea'.

Green Turtle

Chelonia mydas

A few decades ago green turtles used to haul themselves up onto Dubai beaches by the dozen to lay their eggs. Now their nesting grounds are covered by harbours, hotels and high rises, and their breeding sites are restricted to some of the offshore islands. Although five species of sea turtle have been recorded in the region, only the green turtle and the hawksbill turtle breed here. The breeding season runs from May to August..

ENVIRONMENT AND THE LAW

The UAE's enthusiasm for developments is understandable, but it leads to conflict between construction projects and the need to conserve the country's natural resources. However, many agencies are working on nature's side, and the Federal Law for Environmental Development and Protection regulates fishing and navigation activities with the aim of protecting marine life and water resources in the UAE.

Established in 1996, the Environment Agency Abu Dhabi (EAD) is committed to protecting and enhancing air quality, groundwater and desert and marine ecosystems and has several important projects underway. In 2013, the EAD implemented a Marine Water Quality Protection Plan, and in August 2014, together with Abu Dhabi Tourism and Culture Authority, published a new guide, *Management of Beach Water Quality for Human Health at Abu Dhabi Hotels*.

Abu Dhabi Global Environmental Data Initiative (AGEDI) is actively monitoring environmental conditions in the emirate. One of its projects, the Abu Dhabi Blue Carbon Demonstration Project, aims to improve the understanding of coastal ecosystems and how they help to sequester carbon and provide valuable services to coastal communities.

The UAE is also party to international agreements on biodiversity, climate change, desertification, endangered species, hazardous wastes, marine dumping and ozone layer protection.

Despite the efforts being made, there are some serious environmental issues facing the UAE. The massive scale of development in Dubai on gigantic projects such as the three Palm Islands, the World and Dubai Waterfront, is changing the coastline of Dubai and its ecosystem permanently (see Life Under The Palms.

Conservationists say that the massive construction in the Arabian Gulf is damaging breeding grounds for the endangered hawksbill turtle, as well as destroying coral reefs and fish stocks. The developers, however, argue that the sites attract sealife, and point to the increases in fish and marine life around the crescent on Palm Jumeirah.

Marine Protected Areas

The website protectedplanet.net states that the UAE has 25 protected areas (PAs); 12 of which are marine areas, and 13 terrestrial. The figures vary depending on who you consult, but the UAE is attempting to preserve both land and sea. In Abu Dhabi alone there is currently a proposal to declare four new protected zones.

In marine PAs, fishing, and coral or shell collecting is prohibited. Although there are signs explaining this, the rules are often ignored.

But marine life in the UAE is tough. According to experts in water resources and nature conservation at the UAE's Ministry of Environment and Water, sea life in the Gulf is very resilient due to having to adapt to the extreme heat (35°C in summer) and high salinity of the water.

As awareness of marine conservation grows, there are more programmes to protect marine life, such as the rehabilitation of mangroves, coral reef planting, and the expansion of critical habitats for marine life.

The Marawah Marine in Abu Dhabi is one of the largest protected areas in the Gulf. Its sea grass beds, dugongs and turtles make it an important resource.

Dugongs and Turtles

Dugongs, hawksbill and green turtles make up some of the UAE's most ecologically important, and endangered, marine species. Dugongs are listed as vulnerable to extinction, while hawksbill turtles are listed as critically endangered and green turtles as endangered.

The Arabian Gulf and Red Sea are said to be home to a population of more than 5,000 dugongs; the largest population of these creatures outside of Australia. Of these, about 40% are found in the waters off the UAE, specifically off Abu Dhabi.

While dugongs and turtles are protected under federal law, they are constantly under threat. Gill net fishing, especially the use of drift nets, is said to be the main cause of death among the UAE's dugongs, though laws have been put in place banning such fishing in certain areas where dugongs are known to forage. The second biggest threat to a dugong is being hit by a boat.

Dugongs and turtles are also threatened by the damage that's being done to their habitats and breeding grounds through coastal development, dredging and pollution. When turtles come ashore to lay their eggs, they are easily disturbed by people and vehicle movement, and their nests are vulnerable to predation by people and feral dogs.

While there are projects such as the Dubai Turtle Rehabilitation Project (DTRP), which nurtures sick and injured turtles back to health before releasing them back into the wild, the impact man is having on turtles is still devastating. Emirates Wildlife Society-WWF project manager Moaz Sawaf reluctantly reported in 2014 that turtle numbers were still decreasing in the UAE.

DID YOU KNOW?

- 60% of marine rubbish consists of plastic – bags, sweet wrappers, bottles, straws and the like
- Cigarette butts have been found in the stomachs of fish, whales and turtles
- It takes more than 12 years for a cigarette butt to disintegrate

	Hawksbill Turtle	Green Turtle
Length	55-95cm	80-120cm
Weight	About 55kg	130-250kg
Habitat	Reefs and rocky areas	Inlets and bays
Diet	Sea urchins, sponges, molluscs and sea squirts	
Status	Critically endangered	Endangered
Identifying features	Narrow upper jaw with a distinctive overbite. Two claws on each front flipper. The scales (or scutes) on their shells overlap	Serrated jaw. One claw on each front flipper

ENVIRONMENTAL ACTION

Divers are usually environmentally conscious – they like looking at marine life, and so it pays to help preserve it. Look, but don't touch is most divers' policy.

If you feel strongly about the environment, why not do something about it? You can contact one of the environmental groups in the UAE – they always need volunteers and funds. Playing an active role in protecting the underwater environment will also increase the pleasure you get from diving.

Emirates Diving Association

The Emirates Diving Association is a non-profit organisation, accredited by the United Nations Environment Programme, that consists of a handful of volunteers who share a passion for the marine environment. It has signed a memorandum of understanding with the UAE Ministry of Environment and Water to protect the UAE's shoreline and reefs. EDA also actively drives various conservation projects such as a reef monitoring programme and clean-ups of dive sites, and it arranges dive trips. Contact EDA on 04 393 9390 or visit emiratesdiving.com.

Emirates Environmental Group

This is a voluntary, non-governmental organisation devoted to protecting the environment in general through education, action programmes and community involvement. Activities include evening lectures on environmental topics, recycling collections and clean-up campaigns. Annual membership costs Dhs.300 for adults and Dhs.100 for students. Contact them on 04 344 8622 or visit eeg-uae.org or facebook.com/EmiratesEnvironmentalGroup.

ECO-DIVING PRACTICES

On an individual level, every diver can do their bit towards protecting or preserving the marine environment.

- Don't remove any creatures – even if they appear to be dead.
- Don't 'ride' turtles – they will panic and drown.
- Don't touch any marine creature: they could be harmful, they could be harmed and they will certainly be scared off. It's far more satisfying to observe them going about their daily routines.
- Don't touch corals. Hard corals are made up of millions of zooxanthellae, which they need to grow and to form the foundation of their limestone skeleton. Soft corals consist of delicate polyps. If you touch them, you'll kill them. In addition, coral cuts are notoriously likely to become infected and take a long time to heal.
- Don't litter or dump rubbish.
- When you're out on a dive, do your fellow divers and the marine environment a favour and collect any litter you find. Empty plastic bags, cans, old bottles and discarded fishing nets can kill marine life (but check that there aren't any creatures inside them before removing them from the site).
- Maintain your buoyancy – this means you're less likely to crash into any delicate corals.
- Take care when anchoring.
- If you have a picnic on the beach, throw your rubbish away in the bins provided or, better still, take it away with you.

DIVING

A couple of things are really important to divers: their training, gear, health... and a good insurance policy. And once all the basics are in place, you can then start to broaden your underwater horizons.

Training

Most people are curious about the underwater world, but they're also understandably nervous about the idea of breathing underwater. Fortunately, most courses are well-structured and easy-to-follow and will take you from apprehensive to advanced in no time.

In order to be able to dive anywhere in the world, you must complete, and pass, an open water diver course from any one of the reputable training organisations – BSAC, CMAS, NAUI, PADI, SSI and SDI. (Of these, PADI is the largest, and the one you're most likely to encounter.) As proof of this, you'll receive a certification card (a 'C-card') which allows you to go on an 'open water' rated dive of up to 18m in depth.

A good dive school will then encourage you to go on a few pleasure dives with an instructor: this will help you to build confidence and apply the skills you've learnt. The aim is to make those skills a reflex action so you feel comfortable enough in the water to start wondering about what's next. (For a list of schools, see the Dive Directory.)

What's next is advanced diver training. A dive agency generally packages a few courses that focus on specific skills together. (See the tip box opposite to see what a PADI advanced programme consists of. Other dive agencies will offer something similar.) This is a good way for you to upgrade your skills and explore aspects of diving that are of particular interest to you, but there's no real industry standard as to what makes an advanced diver.

Basically your advanced course will end with you feeling well-versed in many of the less exciting, but nevertheless important aspects of diving, such as dive planning, navigation, using a dive computer, boat dives, dealing with currents and safety procedures. You'll also have an opportunity to do more of the stuff that really interests you, be it diving on wrecks, diving at night or learning more about the life you'll see down there.

Once you've got an advanced diver certification, you'll find there is still plenty more to do. It's a good idea to complete a rescue and first aid course, for example. And then, if this is where your interests lie, you'll be ready to take on the more technical side of diving, such as diving on Nitrox and going to depths of 30 to 40m, which is the generally accepted recreational diving limit.

Technical Diving

There are various definitions of technical diving, but most diving organisations agree that diving becomes technical when you go beyond the recreational diving limit of 40m or exceed the conventional limits of recreational diving.

In technical diving you use mixed gases to increase your bottom time or, in extreme technical diving, replace them with inert gases to lower the risks.

As it might suggest, technical diving involves far more complicated equipment, which is a sizeable investment. Dive planning also takes on a whole new meaning, and you're going to have to be a lot more committed to the sport than a recreational diver. Your fitness becomes more important as you deal with increased time in the water and the weight of your gear. In other words, technical diving takes you way beyond recreational diving. It's not for everyone, but for enthusiasts the ability to reach new depths is exhilarating.

For more information on this type of diving, contact the Technical Diving International Center, or Coastal Technical Divers (details in the Dive Directory).

Never attempt to dive for deeper or longer than you are qualified to do; technical diving is much riskier than recreational diving.

A PADI ADVANCED OPEN WATER PROGRAMME

PADI offers the following 'Adventures in Diving' programme, but most agencies offer a similar set of options, prerequisites and qualifications.

What do you need?

Open water diver or qualifying certification from PADI or any other recognised organisation. You have to be at least 15 years old (or 12 for the PADI Junior Advanced Open Water Diver).

What does the course involve?

The course includes deep diving, underwater navigation and a choice of three from the following: Altitude Diver, Boat Diver, Deep Diver, Diver Propulsion Vehicle, Drift Diver, Dry Suit Diver, Multilevel Diver, Night Diver, Peak Performance Buoyancy, Search and Recovery Diver, Underwater Naturalist, Underwater Navigator, Underwater Photographer, Underwater Videographer, AWARE Fish Identification or Wreck Diver.

The course requires at least 15 hours of lessons and you'll complete a minimum of five dives over two days.

Then what?

You can now sign up for dives that require your new set of skills, and you can enroll in further speciality courses such as rescue, deep or wreck diving or underwater photography.

EQUIPMENT

With diving being such a popular sport in the UAE, it's easy to buy good diving gear. For a full list of dive gear suppliers, see the Dive Directory.

Entry-level dive gear or snorkelling kits are generally widely available in the UAE. Go Sports, for example, stocks a range of Mares and Cressi gear from fins and masks to regulators and wetsuits.

Al Boom Diving (the diving section of Al Boom Marine, previously Scuba Dubai) sells Cressi gear and does airfills and servicing. Mohammed Bin Masaood & Sons exclusively sells and services Mares gear, but doesn't do airfills. Gulf Marine Sports sells a variety of diving equipment.

Many of your dives here will be done as part of a group and you'll go out to the site by boat. Seeing as most dive gear is pretty uniform (black neoprene with possibly a splash of colour), it makes sense to mark your gear so that you'll be able to spot it quickly on a dive boat or in a dive centre when everyone is kitting up.

Rinsing your gear off well in cold, desalinated water after each dive is a must, and the climate requires that you need to do gear maintenance checks more frequently than you might elsewhere.

Temp.	Protection
30°C+	Lycra or 0.5mm suit for protection from the sun, hydrocorals and jellyfish
26-29°C	0.5mm suit or 2.5mm shortie wetsuit for a little protection
23-25°C	3mm one or two piece suit consisting of farmer john and jacket
18-22°C	5mm one or two piece suit consisting of farmer john and jacket
18°C	5 or 7mm semi- or dry suit

Suiting Up for Gulf Diving

While Gulf waters are typically warm, every diver has different tolerance levels

BREATHE RIGHT

If you haven't been diving in a while, it's a really good idea to have your regulator serviced before you get back into the water. Also, always take care to rinse your reg thoroughly after a dive and make sure that you put the dust cap on once you've disconnected it from the cylinder.

for the cold and you'll feel even chillier if you're doing repetitive dives, long dives or deep dives.

How thick you want your wetsuit to be also depends on the time of year you're going diving (see the Water Temperatures table). If you get cold easily or are doing a deep dive, wearing a hood could be your best bet. Up to 30% of your body heat is lost through your head, so it's not surprising to find that a hood makes a huge difference. The temperature table opposite provides some guidelines to help you choose what degree of protection you will need. Don't forget, the thicker the wetsuit, the more buoyant you are and the more weight you will need.

Water Temperatures

Below is a table of monthly average water temperatures, given in Celsius, for the southern Arabian Gulf, the east coast and Musandam. However, temperatures are often affected by unpredictable thermoclines that result from cold water flowing in from the Indian Ocean.

Months	Arabian Gulf	East Coast & Musandam
January	18 - 23	21 - 23
February	20 - 23	20 - 23
March	20 - 25	20 - 24
April	24 - 26	22 - 24
May	27 - 30	22 - 27
June	27 - 32	23 - 27
July	31 - 35	28 - 30
August	33 - 36	32 - 30
September	30 - 33	31 - 29
October	30 - 33	30 - 27
November	25 - 30	29 - 26
December	23 - 25	26 - 23

HEAVY METAL

European rules state that a visual inspection of your cylinder, whether it's a stainless steel or aluminium one, is required every two-and-a-half years. In the Gulf however, due to the heat, humidity and high salinity, it's recommended that your cylinders receive a visual inspection once a year, and that they are hydro-tested every five years.

UNDERWATER PHOTOGRAPHY

Once you can dive, you'll want to photograph the colourful marine life. But, as soon as you head underwater colour is lost; starting with the reds and oranges and followed by yellows and greens. You'll need to bring out the colour of the reef life by using a strobe. This will allow the true beauty of the underwater realm to dazzle.

Composition is also important. You'll need to fill the frame as much as possible with your subject, which means getting as close to it as you can. To add to the challenge you also generally need to try and shoot your subject from below rather than above – camouflage is how most creatures under the water make it to old age, but it also greatly increases the difficulties an underwater photographer faces. Many wide-angle images don't look like much to anyone, even the most enthusiastic diver, without a human subject in them. A hole in a wreck isn't all that exciting. Frame your dive buddy in that hole to show how big or small it is and this will give your shot a lot more impact.

Your dive buddy is essential for reasons other than posing for shots. They can help you position your strobe to best effect, keep an eye on you and remind you of your dive profile, depth, time and air when you're likely to be caught up in the excitement of taking photographs.

Cameras and Housings

There are two options when it comes to buying cameras and housings. You can choose an all-in-one system of an amphibious camera complete with interchangeable lenses, a choice of strobes and other accessories. These, like the Sea&Sea MX10, Motormarine II or Nikonos V, are excellent choices for beginners.

Alternatively, you could use a standard camera housed in a watertight case. You

will still need to buy a port and gears for the lens, plus strobes. A digital camera and underwater housing costs around Dhs.2,700 and a JVC video camera and housing will cost about Dhs.5,200.

Canon's headquarters are on Sheikh Zayed Road opposite Times Square Center, and Sony brand equipment is available from Jumbo Stores. Al Boom Diving sells a limited selection of camera housings. Ikelite and Subal are specialist housing systems and they are available for most of the high-end point and shoot as well as SLR camera brands, such as Nikon, Canon, Olympus, Sony, Fuji and Kodak.

You can also rent an underwater camera for about Dhs.250 per day or a video camera for around Dhs.350 per day from most of the dive centres.

Photographic Courses

PADI Digital Underwater Photography and Videographer courses for snorkellers and certified divers are available at most of the PADI dive centres. They cover the basics of the equipment you need to use, camera preparation, photographic techniques, colour, composition, resolution settings and downloading images.

The photographer course costs about Dhs.1,250 – 1,550 and the videographer course is about Dhs.1,625. The courses include two sea dives, use of camera equipment, computer equipment and burning a CD of your first images. Costs will depend on whether you have your own equipment or use the dive centre's gear, which is recommended initially.

PHOTOGRAPHY CHECKLIST

- ☐ Use the camera on land to familiarise yourself with it
- ☐ Check that the batteries are charged (and check strobe batteries)
- ☐ Check camera settings prior to your dive
- ☐ Leak test the housing prior to entering the sea
- ☐ Get close to your subject and try different settings
- ☐ Rinse the camera and housing in fresh water after the dive
- ☐ Ensure the camera is completely dry before opening the housing and downloading the results or removing the film
- ☐ Reload fresh batteries, insert the memory card and regrease the o-rings as necessary

FITNESS AND INSURANCE

Always have the number of the nearest diving doctor and a hotline to a recompression chamber – just in case.

Before you can sign up for a course, your dive school will request that you complete a form regarding your general health. If you reply yes to any of the questions on it, you will be required to obtain a certificate from a doctor stating that you're fit enough to dive and that you don't have any conditions, such as asthma or epilepsy, that would prevent you from diving.

When it comes to insurance, sport diving is in a category of its own. If you dive regularly an annual insurance policy offers value for money. Check if there's a limit on the number or length of the trips you can take, if there's any excess to be paid, whether there's a limit on the depth, number or types of dives you can do and if hyperbaric treatment is covered.

Divers Alert Network (DAN) is a non-profit medical and research organisation that provides medical information, diving insurance and emergency assistance. DAN is familiar to most divers – which isn't surprising considering it's the largest global diver organisation. DAN membership entitles you to 24 hour medical assistance in the event of a medical emergency, worldwide. This means that if you find yourself in trouble, DAN will organise medical transport, coordinate hyperbaric and medical treatment, refer you to medical specialists and assist with travel arrangements for you or a family member.

Insurance through DAN is specific to diving, valid worldwide and there are no excess fees. It also covers your travel and dive gear. And, seeing as you hopefully may not ever need DAN's assistance, you'll still receive benefits in the form of a subscription to their magazine, special offers and access to seminars and

EMERGENCY NUMBERS

Dubai Police
Rescue Department 999

Diving Physicians
Dr Barbara Karin Vela, Dubai, 050 885 8172

Dr Mohamed Nawaz, Hyperbaric Doctor, Abu Dhabi, 050 587 5118

Dr Suliman Nayal, Dr Nayal's Clinic, Port Saeed, Dubai, 04 295 9444 (closed during summer)

conferences on underwater safety. A basic membership costs $35 (Dhs.128). There are a number of plans available, including options for dive professionals.

The DAN network consists of five independent, non-profit organisations (DAN America, DAN Europe, DAN Southern Africa, DAN Japan, DAN South East Asia Pacific) that are funded by their members' fees. The UAE and the rest of the Gulf falls under DAN Europe.

The Professional Association of Diving Instructions (PADI) also provides comprehensive dive insurance through HUB International Insurance Services Inc. (previously Vicencia & Buckley). However, if you live outside the US this policy is only available to PADI professional members and members of the PADI Diving Society. Apply through its website (diveinsurance.com) to see annual fees.

Why Diving and Dentists Go Together

Keep teeth in good health because there are three main problems divers can encounter when submerged: muscle or joint pain, tooth squeeze and pain caused by ill-fitting dentures. Also, check with your dentist if new or temporary fillings will be OK to dive with.

RECOMPRESSION

Diving is a safe sport, but there is always a risk of decompression sickness if a diver stays too deep for too long or ascends too rapidly. One of the first symptoms is aches and pains in the joints, and following that there may be a skin rash or dizziness and other neurological symptoms. If you notice any of these symptoms after diving, consult a doctor immediately – it is likely that you will need oxygen and possibly a hyperbaric recompression chamber urgently.

Before you can receive treatment in a recompression chamber, a qualified diving doctor MUST sign a consent form. In Dubai you can contact Dr Barbara Karin Vela for diving-related questions at Dubai London Clinic and Speciality Hospital on Jumeirah Beach Road in Um Suqeim (800-DLC /800 352) or for emergencies ONLY: 050 885 8172.

The UAE only has two hyperbaric recompression chambers: one at Zayed Military Hospital in Abu Dhabi (02 444 8100); and another at Aqua Marine Diving Services in Al Quoz industrial area in Dubai (04 323 3100 or 04 323 3200).

Aqua Marine Diving support the DAN insurance network and can offer recompression treatment when recommended by a hyperbaric doctor.

DIVE INSURANCE CONTACT DETAILS

DAN Europe
daneurope.org
+39 085 893 0333
mail@daneurope.org

PADI
diveinsurance.com
+714 739 3177

Vicencia & Buckley
comments@diveinsurance.com

ACTIVITIES

Even for non-divers a weekend living on the sea is a wonderful thing. Charter a dhow, throw in your mask and snorkel, and start exploring.

Snorkelling

Snorkelling is a great hobby and with the conditions in the UAE consisting of relatively calm waters for most of the year, this is the perfect place to get into it. Whatever your age or fitness levels, snorkelling will get you into the sea and the minute you get your first glimpse of bright reef life, you'll be hooked.

Thanks to their noisy breathing apparatus, divers often tend to scare many marine animals away, or at least keep their distance. Snorkellers though are well-placed to see excellent fish life. Divers often return to the boat to hear of turtles being seen coming up for air on the surface, rays jumping out of the water (apparently to get parasites off their backs) and of shoals of different fish near the surface. In the winter there are some areas where you're almost guaranteed sightings of sharks and, again, snorkellers often strike it luckier than divers.

Benefits

This is a great way for the family to enjoy an activity together, using only basic equipment. And unlike divers, when snorkellers see something exciting, they can call their buddy over to share the sight.

Equipment

All you need is a tempered glass mask, a snorkel and fins. Fins are either slip-on or strapped on over booties. It's also a good idea to wear a suit or a 'skin' (which is thinner than a wetsuit but still offers UV protection) to prevent sunburn and to offer some protection from jellyfish stings. If you wear a wetsuit you may need to wear a weightbelt too, especially if you like to duck dive down and check things out.

You can buy or hire snorkelling equipment from most dive shops or centres (see Dive Directory) and some hotels. A good dive shop will advise you on how to find a mask and fins that are a good fit.

Cost

Snorkelling doesn't require expensive equipment. Masks, snorkels and fins range in price from Dhs.100 for a generic set to Dhs.550 for a branded, diving-specific set.

Getting out to a snorkelling spot can involve some expense, although if you head out from the shore all it costs is a little bit of energy on your part. If you want to go snorkelling on the east coast, there are a number of excellent snorkelling sites and most dive centres will take you out on a dive boat. You can snorkel on the surface, or chill out on a nearby island beach, while the divers head down under. Prices vary but you can expect to pay around Dhs.180 for a two-hour trip or so (that's two hours in which you're taken to the site, get to snorkel around it and head back to shore again).

Marine Life

You will see large shoals of reef fish, turtles, rays and even (small) sharks. Don't overlook the corals though: if you take a torch you'll be able to see them in their true colours and the display is amazing.

TRY AND BUY

Dubai-based snorkellers love Al Boom Diving. You can hire equipment on a Thursday and return it on a Saturday from its Al Qouz branch (because they are closed on Fridays), and you're only charged for one day's hire. You can also hire kit before you buy. If you decide to purchase it, they'll give you the cost of the hire off the price of the item.

Snorkelling Sites

West Coast

The only places to snorkel on the west coast are off the harbour walls, but take care: on the outside harbour walls the waves tend to bash against the rocks and you may get caught off guard by a rogue wave. You can snorkel on the inside of the harbour walls, but the water there is rather still and tends to silt up. The fish also prefer the outside walls.

Barracuda Barge (p.8)
Jazirat Sir Bu Na'air (p.28)
Turtle Barge (p.48)

Musandam

Take care when snorkelling in Musandam as there can be unusual currents due to the narrow channel between Oman and Iran (the Strait of Hormuz). It's a good idea to go with a tour company and have a guide to point out the best sites. The best fish life is to be found between the surface and 10m, so try to snorkel along the side of rocks and islands.

There are a number of tour companies that offer dhow trips for dolphin watching and snorkelling. The boats are usually moored in areas that are safe to snorkel in, and you can even arrange overnight camping trips with these companies. Khasab Tours on the Musandam west coast and Al Marsa on the Musandam east coast are some of the operators here (see Dive Directory).

East Coast

The east coast is a great area for snorkelling and has the most diverse marine life. Most dive centres take snorkellers out on their boats (along with divers, and the trip lasts for about two hours in total). Some centres can make arrangements to take you to Shark or Khor Fakkan Island where you can spend the day. They'll come and collect at the time you agree on. If that's what you'd like to do, it's best to arrange this with your dive centre in advance. Depending on your swimming ability and the water conditions, you can go to Sandy Beach Motel (Dhs.75 for adults and Dhs.45 for children to enter if not staying at the hotel) and spend the day on the beach and swim out to Snoopy Island, just a short distance from shore. In winter the water recedes a long way and the distance you have to swim is even less.

Musandam
The Caves (p.68)
Lima Rock (p.72)
Octopus Rock (p.88)
Pearl Island (p.90)
Ras Hamra (p.92)
Ras Lima (p.94)
Ras Marovi (p.96)

East Coast
Dibba Island (p.110)
Hole in the Wall (p.112)
Martini Rock (p.128)
Murbah Reef (p.130)
Ras Qidfa (p.132)
Shark Island (p.136)
Sharm Rocks (p.138)
Snoopy Island (p.140)

SAFETY

- Learn how to breath out strongly so that you can expel water from your snorkel.
- If you're a weak swimmer, snorkel in pairs.
- Look out for boats or jetskis, as they won't see you.
- Use plenty of suncream, but allow it to soak in before you enter the water. If it washes off, not only will you burn, but it will damage the coral.
- Protect against possible jellyfish stings (and sunburn) by wearing a wetsuit.
- Drink plenty of water to prevent dehydration.

Boat, Yacht and Dhow Charters

Sailing along the coast in a dhow is an atmospheric and memorable way to experience the region's coastal life.

There are a number of companies that offer dhow, boat or yacht charters. They range from a sundowner cruise of a couple of hours, overnight trips with stopovers for snorkelling to liveaboard dive excursions. Prices are approximately Dhs.350 per person for one day (dhow cruise only), and Dhs.1,910 per person including a diving trip for two nights.

If you want to do your own thing, large independent groups can charter a dhow from the fishermen at Dibba on the east coast, to travel up the coast to Musandam. If you haggle you can usually knock the price down, especially if you know a bit of Arabic – try saying your proposed price followed by 'mafi mushkila' ('no problem').

Expect to pay around Dhs.2,500 per day for a dhow for 20 – 25 people, or Dhs.100 per hour for a smaller vessel. Take your own food and water (and dive gear if diving), as nothing is supplied onboard. The dhows are equipped with ice lockers though, which are suitable for storing supplies. Conditions are basic, but you'll have the freedom to plan your own route through the beautiful fjord-like Musandam scenery from a traditional wooden dhow.

The water in the area is beautifully clear and turtles and dolphins can often be seen from the boat, although sometimes unfavourable weather conditions can seriously reduce visibility for divers.

If you leave from Dibba, Omani visas are not required, even though you enter Omani waters. It's also possible to arrange stops along the coast and it's worth taking camping equipment for the night, although you can sleep on board.

Hire any equipment you may need before you get to Dibba. Non divers in your group can spend the day swimming, snorkelling and soaking up the sun.

Boat, Yacht and Dhow Charter Companies

UAE			
Abu Dhabi	Arabian Divers	+971 2 665 8742	fishabudhabi.com
Dubai	El Mundo	+971 50 551 7406	elmundodubai.com
	Khasab Travel & Tours	+971 4 266 9950	khasabtours.com
Sharjah	Al Marsa Travel & Tourism & Charters	+971 6 544 1232	almarsamusandam.com
Oman			
Dibba	Nomad Ocean Adventures	+968 2683 6069	discovernomad.com
	Sheesa Beach Travel & Tourism	+968 2683 6551	sheesabeach.com
Khasab	Dolphin Khasab Tours	+968 9956 6672	dolphinkhasabtours.com
	Khasab Travel & Tours	+968 2673 0464	khasabtours.com
	Musandam Sea Adventure Tourism	+968 2673 0069	musandam-sea-adventures.com
	Rahal Musandam	+968 2683 7036	rahalmusandam.com

FIRST AID

Hopefully you'll never have any serious (and seriously unpleasant) encounters while out exploring. However, accidents do happen. Here are some basic first aid pointers in case you have a run-in with some marine life.

One excellent reason for not touching anything and keeping your hands to yourself while diving is the number of things down there that can sting or stab you – many of which are also cunningly camouflaged.

Most marine creatures are not aggressive and would rather flee than attack, but if you unwittingly threaten them by standing on them, touching them or venturing into their territory (or even, sometimes, by trying to take a photograph of them!) the result can be a painful and potentially serious injury.

ALL THE SMALL THINGS

Many tiny things, that you probably haven't even noticed touching, can cause irritation, itchiness or a rash. For example, an attractive coral that looks like a fern or fan is a hydrocoral that can actually deliver a nasty burn, especially if you happen to be susceptible to it. There can also be small pieces of detached jellyfish tentacles that will prickle your skin.

If you're the kind of person who suffers an allergic reaction to bee stings, ant bites or jellyfish, it's wise to steer clear of everything in the water, keep a first aid kit on land, and always wear protection in the water in the form of a wetsuit, even in the summer months. If you don't manage to avoid contact with things that sting and you develop a mild reaction, you can try applying antihistamine or steroid creams to treat the itch or irritation.

Here's a brief guide to dealing with hazardous marine life. For a full picture, it's best to refer to a comprehensive first aid book – you'll find a list of books in the Bibliography. Bites and stings can be serious, and you often don't know exactly what you've been bitten or stung by. When you're unsure, seek medical assistance immediately. Turn to the Directory for a list of emergency contact numbers.

Catfish

Catfish have three spines attached to their dorsal and lateral fins. They're not aggressive and won't attack but they are dangerous to touch.

- Control bleeding
- Immobilise limb
- Medical attention or hospitalisation may be required

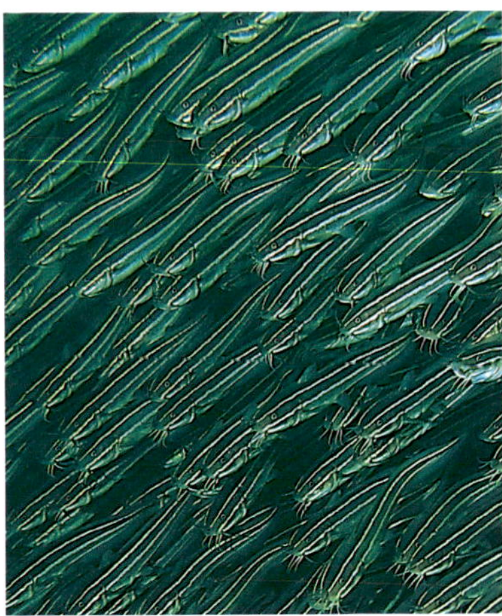

Cone Shell

During the day, most cone shells bury themselves in the sand, emerging at night to search for food. Their weapon is a harpoon-like poison dart that they 'fire' when they spot a potential meal, which injects into the victim. Each shell has a number of harpoons, which are made of a hard, bone-like substance and measure about a centimetre in length. You're most likely to be stung by a cone shell if you pick it up. Cone shells occur on the west, east and Musandam coasts.

Of the hundreds of species of cone shells, only a few are believed to be dangerous. The effect can range from painless, to excruciating with muscle paralysis. Salt water exacerbates the pain.

- Apply pressure bandages, painkillers and CPR
- Wash the wound with hot water (45-50°C) – the wound will have a milky appearance
- Immobilise the limb
- Heart failure can occur in severe cases – so seek medical attention immediately

Crown of Thorns Starfish

These starfish measure up to 60cm in diameter and have 13 to 16 arms covered in sharp spines that can inflict a painful wound. They prey on corals and are usually found in deeper water than other starfish. The spines can cause bleeding, inflammation and secondary infection. If the spines aren't removed the symptoms can continue for weeks or months.

- Immerse wound in water as hot as the victim can stand for 30-90 minutes
- Immobilise or make the victim lie down
- Remove the spines
- In serious cases the broken-off spines may have to be surgically removed

Flower Urchin (Toxopneustes)

While the black spiny urchin is the most common type of urchin and more likely

to cause injury thanks to its longer spines, its cousin the flower urchin is far more dangerous. It looks like it's covered in flowers, but these are actually tiny pincers that pack a venomous punch.

- Wash wound with hot water (45-50°C)
- Immobilise limb or lay victim down
- Remove spines
- Seek medical attention immediately

Hydroid Coral

Hydroid corals look like feathery plants, but they're actually colonies of animals that contain nematocysts (stinging cells) that they use to capture their next meal, and for defence. Divers are particularly prone to brushing against these corals and you'll

want to avoid the fine white feathery ones and the dense yellow-brown types in particular. The sting is irritating and painful, but generally not serious.

- Apply vinegar or alcohol spirit

Jellyfish

There are thousands of marine species that use nematocysts (stinging capsules) as a defence – including corals, anemones and jellyfish.

Contact with a jellyfish can result in anything from a mild, localised itch, to severe burning and throbbing pain or even cardio-respiratory difficulties. It's difficult to know which jellyfish is dangerous and which isn't, but one school of thought is that coloured jellyfish (that appear in September and October in particular) have a bad sting. The extremely dangerous boxfish or deadly sea wasp don't occur in Gulf waters.

- Do not rub wound
- Remove tentacles
- Wash surface of the wound
- Apply ice pack, then vinegar, ammonia or alcohol spirit
- In rare cases, severe stings have arrested breathing and caused heart failure – seek medical attention

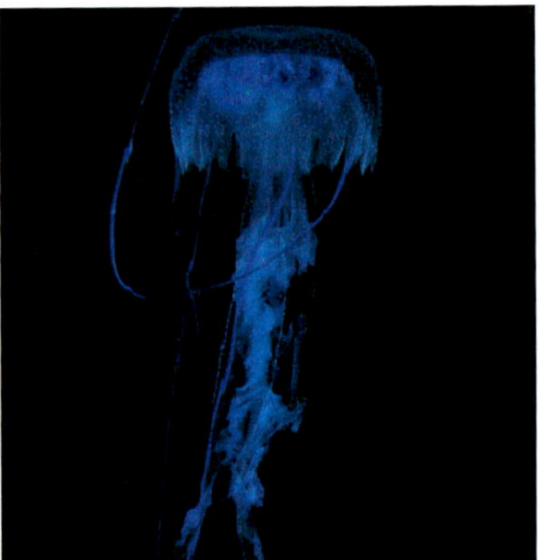

Lionfish

These beautiful fish are not aggressive, although they can be territorial at times. Their long spines contain venom that causes intense pain.

You're most likely to be accidentally hurt by putting your hand into crevices or not watching where you place your hands while exploring a reef – lionfish particularly enjoy the shelter of an overhang, which makes them difficult to spot.

- Wash wound with hot water (45-50°C)
- Control bleeding

- Administer painkillers
- Venom causes intense pain and breathing difficulties – seek medical attention immediately

Moray Eel

These rather scary looking creatures can grow to 2.5m long, and their razor sharp teeth mean a bite will bleed profusely and often becomes infected. But morays aren't aggressive. They can become territorial though, and object to being teased.

- Apply pressure bandages and painkillers
- Control the bleeding
- Immobilise the limb
- As serious secondary infection can occur, hospitalisation is required

Nematocyst

Nematocysts are stinging cells or capsules used by marine creatures like coral, jellyfish and anemones. Some nudibranch species feed on nematocysts and incorporate the effects into their own defence system. The symptoms range from mild skin irritation to intense pain. If a large patch of the skin is exposed, the victim could suffer from nausea and vomiting.

- Gently remove any nematocysts that may still be stuck to the skin (don't squeeze them as this will discharge more nematocysts)
- Apply local anaesthetic spray or ointment
- If breathing becomes impaired seek medical attention
- Give CPR if needed
- Victims might experience intense itching a few days after the event – a steroid cream might help

Octopus

Octopus are not aggressive. Divers only get attacked by them if they accidentally step on them, or pick them up.

Octopus have a break that they use to hunt and defend themselves, and they can inject a mild venom.

- Milk wound
- Immerse limb in hot water
- Apply pressure bandages
- Immobilise limb and keep it lower than the head and heart
- Administer CPR if necessary and seek medical attention immediately

DIVE MEDICAL KIT

Cuts & Wounds
Adhesive dressing and tape, plasters, antiseptic cream

Dehydration
Salt sachet (e.g. Dioralyte), isotonic drinks, water

Marine Stings
Vinegar, sodium bicarbonate, powdered meat tenderiser or any powder

Seasickness
Sturgeron, Dezinil or Dramamine

General
Tweezers, scissors, sterile or saline water, personal medication

Stingray

Stingrays aren't aggressive but can cause excruciating pain if accidentally stepped on, or handled (when fishermen remove them from their nets, for instance). They lie on or near the bottom of the sea and often submerge themselves in the sand. If given half the chance, a ray will swim off, so to avoid stepping on one when you go swimming, shuffle your feet in shallow water, warning them of your approach. The sting can cause deep lacerations and profuse bleeding.

- Apply pressure bandage to stop bleeding (this may take a while)
- Immerse limb in hot water
- Seek medical attention immediately
- Make sure the patient has a tetanus shot if their last one was more than five years previously
- Secondary infection can occur after 24 hours – if the wound becomes more red and painful see a doctor

Scorpionfish

Like stonefish, many scorpionfish look like rocks and they also have venomous spines. They're most likely to cause injury if stepped on or picked up. Although not as dangerous as stonefish, they should be treated the same way. Their sting can cause breathing difficulties, nausea, vomiting, seizures and paralysis.

- Milk wound
- Immobilise limb

- Apply CPR, pressure bandages
- Administer painkillers
- Make victim lie down or immobilise them
- The sting can cause fatal paralysis and cardiac arrest – you should seek medical attention immediately

AVOIDANCE TACTICS

- Avoid close encounters.
- Watch where you put your hands and be aware of your surroundings.
- Practice buoyancy control.
- Wear protective gear.
- Aim to be a passive observer and don't touch or tease marine life.
- Know your limits – when you're out of your depth (literally, in the case of divers), you're more likely to make clumsy mistakes.
- Avoid holding onto a buoy line without gloves as jellyfish and other stinging creatures can get caught on the line.

Sea Snake

Sea snakes are shy and not likely to attack. They also have very small mouths and aren't able to bite large prey. That said, their poison is 20 times more powerful than that of a cobra, but they inject less of it, if any at all, when they bite. Sea snakes live in all tropical waters, except the Atlantic and they're distinguished from land snakes and eels by a flat tail used for swimming.

- Milk wound
- Apply pressure bandages, CPR
- Immobilise victim or lay them down
- Keep limb lower than head and heart
- The venomous bite can cause fatal paralysis and cardiac arrest – seek medical attention immediately

Sea Urchin

The spines of the sea urchin contain venom so watch where you place your hands or feet, especially on rocky snorkelling or diving sites, or if you're exploring a tidal pool or are diving in a confined space in a tunnel for example.

In the UAE you're most likely to encounter urchins on the east coast. The spines can cause mild to severe pain that lasts for a few hours, and the chances of a secondary infection are high. However, very few fatalities have been reported and these have generally been as a result of respiratory problems.

- Do not rub wound or remove spines as they might break off in the skin
- Wash wound with water as hot as the victim can take it (40-50°C)
- Apply vinegar or alcohol spirit
- In most cases the body will break the spines down and dissolve them, but in rare instances they may need to be removed surgically

Stonefish

A fish with a tough, warty skin, the stonefish is usually the colour of its surroundings so it's difficult to spot, but it's only dangerous if stepped on or caught. The stonefish has 13 dorsal spines and when trodden on, these penetrate the skin, injecting venom into the foot. The pain is excruciating and can last for months. Stonefish tend to occur mostly on the UAE's east coast.

- Remove pieces of spines
- Milk the wound – encouraging bleeding might remove some of the venom
- Wash with hot water and immerse wound for 30-90 minutes if possible.
- Immobilise and elevate the limb
- Apply pressure bandages
- Administer painkillers and immobilise the victim or make them lie down
- The venom can cause fatal paralysis and cardiac arrest – you need to seek medical attention immediately

Sharks

Sharks are not venomous, but are largely feared. We'd like to rectify this misunderstanding: although sharks are aggressive predators, scuba divers are not on their menu. It's only when humans overfish and leave sharks hungry that they may travel closer to shore in search of food.

Most injuries to divers from sharks occur because the diver is feeding the shark. When fed (especially by hand) sharks can become frenzied and may inadvertently chew on a diver. Divers should never feed sharks or other marine life if they want to keep their fingers. Also, feeding wild animals disrupts the natural food chain and teaches animals to rely on humans for food.

Sharks are generally just a little curious if they see divers, and they may nudge you and bump you to determine what you are.

There is little data on the different species of sharks in the UAE's waters, but commonly seen on the east coast and in Musandam, are reef sharks, and bottom-feeding nurse sharks and leopard sharks, none of which are dangerous to humans; they will only bite if they feel threatened.

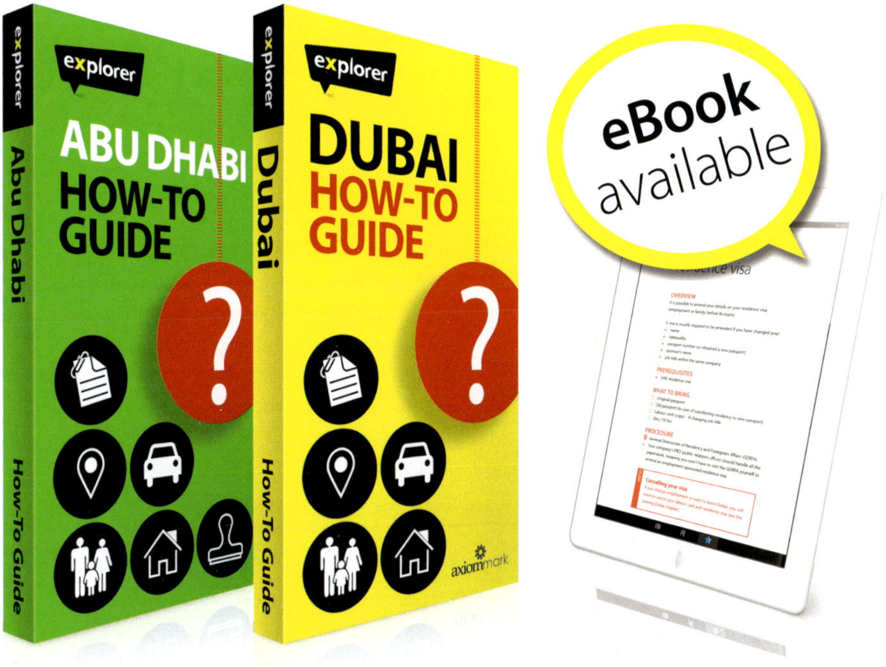

GPS COORDINATES

For the technically-minded, this section is full of the nuts and bolts stuff – from GPS coordinates (and how they are worked out) to wreck data and notes for the historian in you.

The GPS is now the preferred navigation system for divers to find their dive sites. We have given coordinates for all the dive sites covered and many of the popular harbours and launch sites.

Although we now all depend on the GPS receiver, we have also supplied distances and headings to and from dive sites and harbours to assist in dead reckoning navigation in the unlikely event of GPS failure.

Coordinates

The coordinates for each dive site here are given in degrees, minutes and seconds (dd°mm' ss.s").

Map datum

We have used WGS84 (World Geodetic System 84) datum. The map datum affects the relative accuracy between coordinates obtained in one map datum and used in a GPS using a different map datum. All maps have a map datum and there are more than one hundred different data used to accommodate local regional irregularities.

Given the difference it makes, it's important that your GPS receiver is set to the same datum as the coordinates you are entering into it. The difference between one map datum being entered into a GPS received using another map datum, can be as much as 200m.

Most GPS receivers default datum is WGS84. In the set-up of your GPS receiver, you can select regional map data. The Admiralty charts worldwide use WGS84, but it's also useful to know that the UAE regional datum is Nahrwn United Arab Emirates and the Ordnance Survey Great Britain is OSGB.

DIVE SITE COORDINATES

Dive	Name	GPS	Page
WEST COAST			
1	Anchor Barge	N25°30'47.6" E55°04'35.7"	6
2	Barracuda Barge	N25°27'15.6" E55°22'41.4"	8
3	DB1/SMB	N25°16'47.5" E55°03'44.5"	10
4	Energy Determination	N26°04'08.1" E55°34'04.1"	14
5	Hammour Barge	N25°04'40.5" E54°46'06.5"	18
6	Hopper Barge 6	N25°30'27.9" E55°03'58.6"	20
7	Jaramac V	N25°16'49" E55°03'47"	22
8	Jasim	N24°58'47.2" E54°29'43.8"	26
9	Jazirat Sir Bu Na'air	N25°13'30" E54°13'00"	28
10	Lion City	N25°00'13.4" E54°31'43.9"	30
11	Mariam Express	N25°27'19.7" E55°06'16.0"	32
12	MV Dara	N25°34'29.0" E55°27'58.6"	34
13	MV Hannan	N24°50'11.0" E53°53'34.0"	36
14	MV Ludwig	N25°06'53.8" E54°34'14.1"	38
15	Nasteran	N25°28'00.0" E55°21'22.0"	40
16	Neptune 6	N25°30'22.0" E55°03'55.0"	42
17	Swift	N25° 27'37.7" E54° 17'41.2"	46
18	Turtle Barge	N25°26'43.2" E55°26'57.6"	48
19	Victoria Star	N25°24'8.30" E55°16'11.70"	50
20	Zainab	N25°14'55.8" E54°51'32.4"	52
21	Al Dhabiyah Coral Garden	N24°23'60.00" E54° 4'48.00"	55
22	Car Cemetery	N24°16'48.00" E52°39'36.00"	55
23	Gasha Buoy Rig	N24°28'48.00" E53° 6'36.00"	56
24	Hook Island	N24°21'44.14" E52°45'46.10"	56
25	Pearl Wreck	N24°16'48.00" E52°39'36.00"	57
MUSANDAM			
26	The Caves	N25°48'14.4" E56°22'03.0"	68
27	The Landing Craft	N26°12'40.0" E56°17'05.1"	70
28	Lima Rock	N25°56'27.2" E56°27'51.2"	72
29	Bu Rashid	N26°24'12.0" E56°29'42.0"	75
30	Ennerdale Rock	N26°27'39.5" E56°30'57.2"	75
31	Fanaku Island	N26°29'55.1" E56°31'50.4"	76
32	Great Quion Island	N26°30'21.0" E56°30'51.6"	76
33	Hard Rock Cafe	N26°12'13.0" E56°29'18.5"	77
34	Jazirat Al Khayl	N26°22'24.0" E56°26'51.0"	77
35	Jazirat Hamra	N26°16'54.0" E56°27'12.0"	78
36	Jazirat Sawda	N26°17'43.6" E56°27'12.5"	78
37	Jazirat Musandam East Head	N26°22'11.0" E56°32'18.0"	78
38	Jazirat UmmAl Fayyarin	N26°10'31.9" E56°32'47.2"	79
39	Kachalu Island	N26°23'45.5" E56°31'48.1"	79

Dive	Name	GPS	Page
41	Ras Alull	N26°14'51.22" E56°27'46.07"	80
40	Mushroom Rock	N26°17'20.39" E56°27'4.38"	80
42	Ras Arous	N26°14'23.12" E56°28'51.67"	81
43	Ras Bashin	N26°11'5.61" E56°28'31.14"	81
44	Ras Dillah	N26°07'51.0" E56°29'16.2"	82
45	Ras Dillah Ghubbat Ash Shabus Bay	N26° 08' 37.3" E56° 28' 47.1"	82
46	Ras Khaysah South	N26°13'56.38" E56°29'26.03"	83
48	Ras Musandam	N26°23'12.1" E56°31'29.1"	83
47	Ras Khaysah North	N26°14'2.25" E56°29'30.12"	83
49	Ras Qabr Al Hindi	N26°18'33.8" E56°30'52.1"	83
50	Ras Samid	N26° 1'33.19" E56°25'33.13"	84
51	Ras Sarkan	N26°05'17.3" E56°28'18.7"	84
52	Ruqq Suwayk	N26°24'11.9" E56°28'42.1"	85
53	WhiteRock	N26°14'11.9" E56°29'42.6"	85
54	Octopus Rock	N26°00'01.2" E56°26'20.4"	88
55	Pearl Island	N25°57'36.6" E56°25'51.9"	90
56	Ras Hamra	N25°55'20.7" E56°26'38.7"	92
57	Ras Lima	N25°56'46.2" E56°27'30.7"	94
58	Ras Marovi	N25°59'4.26" E56°26'6.68"	96

EAST COAST

Dive	Name	GPS	Page
59	Anemone Gardens	N25°21'01.3" E56°22'46.9"	102
60	Car Cemetery	N25°25'07.0" E56°22'34.2"	104
61	Coral Gardens	N25°21'12.0" E56°22'48.0"	106
62	Deep Reef	N25°04'02.7" E56°24'25.6"	108
63	Dibba Island	N25°36'14.1" E56°21'05.9"	110
64	Hole in the Wall	N25°20'26.3" E56°22'39.7"	112
65	Inchcape 1	N25°30'44.8" E56°22'56.7"	114
66	Inchcape 2	N25°20'19.14" E56°22'52.68"	118
67	Inchcape 10	N25°07'36.1" E56°23'05.3"	124
68	Ines	N25°11'21.8" E56°27'30.6"	126
69	Martini Rock	N25°20'05.2" E56°22'53.0"	128
70	Murbah Reef	N25°16'21.0" E56°22'31.6"	130
71	Ras Qidfa	N25°19'27.2" E56°22'56.0"	132
72	Refinery Reef	N25°18'22.7" E56°23'10.9"	134
73	Shark Island	N25°21'12.0" E56°22'36.2"	136
74	Sharm Rocks	N25°28'55.0" E56°21'57.1"	138
75	Snoopy Island	N25°29'29.0" E56°21'59.0"	140

NOTE:

The map data used in UAE Diving for all dive site coordinates is WGS84, the World Geodetic System 84. Please ensure you select this option in your GPS receiver set-up.

HARBOUR LOCATIONS

WEST COAST

The Club Slipway & Public Slipway, Abu Dhabi

WEST COAST

Umm Suqeim Fishing Harbour, Dubai

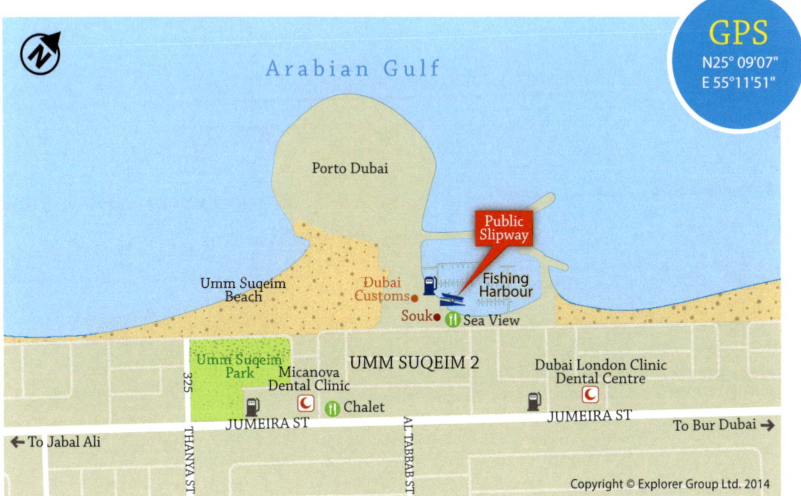

FURTHER INFO
HARBOUR LOCATIONS

WEST COAST
Jebel Ali Hotel Marina, Jabal Ali

WEST COAST
Dubai Creek (Mouth), Dubai

WEST COAST

Dubai International Marine Club (DIMC), Dubai

WEST COAST

Dubai Offshore Sailing Club (DOSC) Harbour , Dubai

WEST COAST

Sharjah Creek, Sharjah

WEST COAST

Hamriyah Harbour, Sharjah

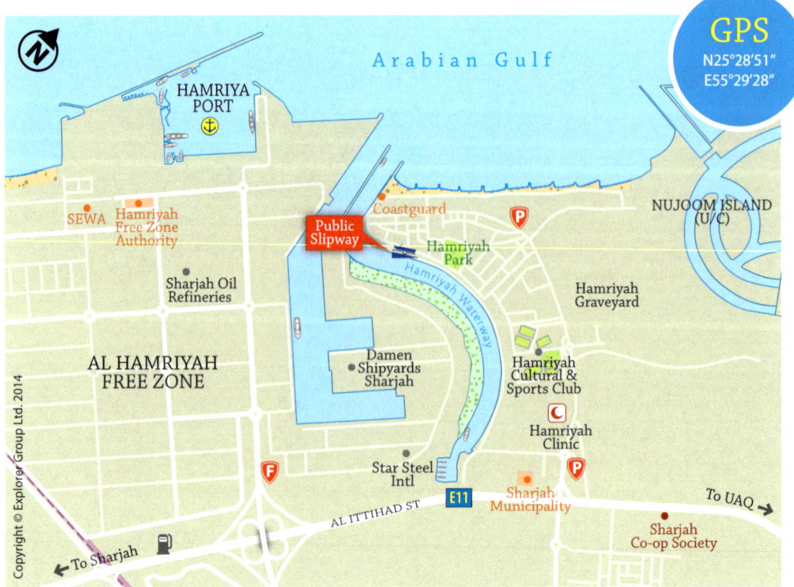

WEST COAST

Dibba Bayah Harbour, Dibba

EAST COAST

Khor Fakkan Harbour Slipway, Khor Fakkan

GPS
N25°20'53"
E56°21'44"

EAST COAST

Lulaya Harbour, Khor Fakkan

GPS
N25°23'37"
E56°22'03"

EAST COAST

Fujairah International Marine Club (FIMC), Fujairah

MUSANDAM

Khasab Port, Khasab

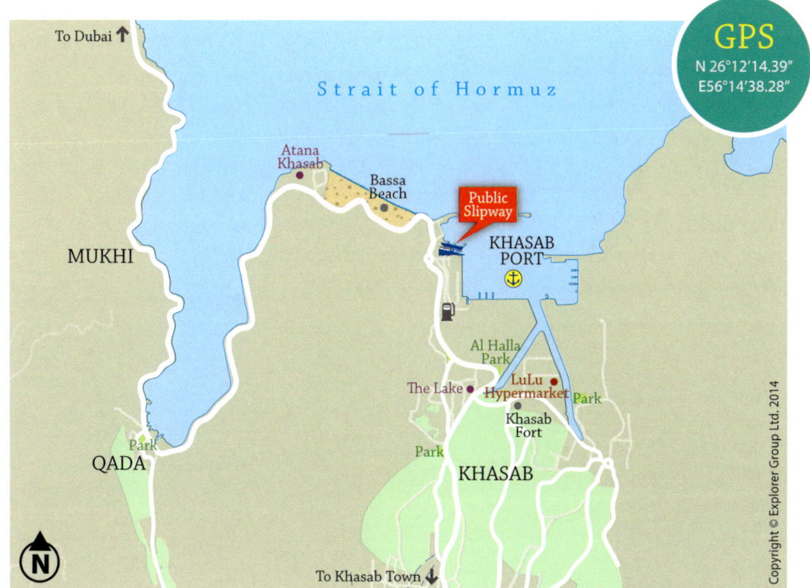

SHIPPING WEIGHTS AND MEASURES

Displacement Tonnage

This is the weight of the water displaced by the boat. It's equal to the weight of the boat and all that is in her; therefore it varies with her draft. Displacement in tonnes = volume of water displaced (in cubic feet), divided by 35 or 36 (depending on whether the water is salt or fresh). Displacement may also be quoted in tonnage.

- 35 cubic feet of salt water weighs 1 tonne
- 36 cubic feet of fresh water weighs 1 tonne
- 1 cubic foot = 0.0283 cubic metres
- 1 cubic metre = 35.31 cubic feet
- 1 tonne = 2,240 pounds or 1,000 kilograms

Dead-weight (DWT)

This is the weight of the cargo, stores, fuel, passengers and crew when the boat is loaded to her maximum summer load line. It's expressed in pounds, tonnes or kilograms.

Gross Tonnage

The gross tonnage measurement is used to determine manning, safety, and other statutory requirements. It is measured according to the law of the national authority with which the vessel is registered. The measurement is the capacity of all the spaces within the hull, and enclosed spaces above the deck available for cargo, stores, passengers and crew (with certain exceptions), divided by 100. The amount is expressed in cubic feet.

Net Tonnage

This figure is derived by deducting the space used for the accommodation of the crew, navigation equipment, machinery and fuel from the figure for the vessel's gross tonnage.

Builder's Measure

Until 1873, the tonnage of a vessel was called Builder's Measurement (BM). This was more than likely based on the number of casks the vessel could carry. After 1873, displacement tonnage was used. From about 1926, the actual weight has been calibrated. Data on some vessels is shown in BM, but over time this number has been converted to actual tonnes and may not be precise – in other words, a vessel shown as 100BM is not automatically 100 tonnes.

DIMENSIONS

Length (L) – length from stern to bow
Breadth (B) – length of beam from port to starboard
Depth (D) – depth from deck to keel
Height (H) – height from keel to the top of the bridge

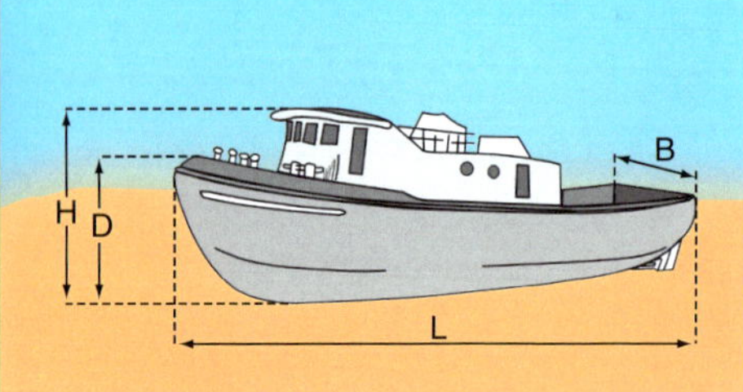

WRECK DATA

Wherever possible we have supplied information about each wreck. Data has been obtained either from the Lloyd's Register of Shipping or from the Hydrographic List.

Lloyd's List

Up until 1741, there was no centralised source of information on shipwrecks. Details were kept locally, and information on a limited number of incidents was traceable through secondary sources, such as a checklist of narratives of shipwrecks and disasters at sea.

A daily record on information on shipping casualties is available from 1741, the year of the oldest surviving issue of the Lloyd's List. As the Lloyd's of London's intelligence network grew, so the List became increasingly comprehensive, covering not only British vessels and wrecks in British waters, but shipping losses worldwide.

From 1856 onwards, reports of enquiries were also published in newspapers, most notably Mitchell's Maritime Register, 1856-1884, and the Shipping Gazette (Lloyd's List Weekly Summary).

A variety of indexes is available from the Guildhall Library in London. These and other records of losses are described in the second edition of the Guide to the Lloyd's Marine Collection by Declan Barriskill.

'Posted' editions of the Lloyd's Register of Ships often indicated the fate of a vessel – 'collision', 'foundered', 'condemned' or so on. Sometimes the year and the month are added (3.89) and refer to the relevant quarter of the Lloyd's Register Casualty Return, published from 1890 to date. The Casualty Returns are available for research at Lloyd's Register in London.

The Mercantile Navy List is never posted but, from 1875 to 1904 lists of vessels removed from the British register are included, with brief reasons why. Separate monthly returns that listed vessels added or removed were also printed. The Public Records Office in Surrey, UK, has bound volumes of these for the period 1875 to 1890 while the Guildhall Library has them for 1890 to 1946. These are particularly useful for vessels not actually lost at sea, but hulked, laid up or condemned.

Wreck Register	The number allocated to the wreck by Lloyd's or the Hydrographic Society
Name	The original name of the vessel
Nationality	The name of the country or flag that the boat sailed under
Year Built	The year the vessel was built
Type	The boat may have been one of the following types: cargo vessel, coastal barge, coastal tanker, coastal vessel, landing craft, motor lighter, passenger liner, tug, very large crude container
Tonnage	Refer to information on Shipping Weights and Measures (opposite)
Cargo	What the boat was carrying at the time of loss

GLOSSARY

Aft	The area towards the stern of the boat
Beam	The greatest width of the boat
Bow	The area towards the front of the boat
Bridge	The location from which a vessel is steered and its speed controlled
Bulkhead	A vertical partition separating compartments
Buoy	An anchored float used for marking a mooring or position in the water
Deck	A permanent covering over a compartment, hull or any part thereof
Draft	The depth of water a boat draws
DSMB	Delayed Surface Marker Buoy, an inflatable buoy used by scuba divers to show where they are. It can be inflated under water, usually at the end of a dive
DWT	Dead-weight
GPS	Global positioning system (satellite navigation system)
Hatch	An opening in a boat's deck, fitted with a watertight cover
Hold	A compartment below deck in a large vessel, used solely for cargo
Hull	The main body of a vessel
LC	Landing craft
MV	Motor vessel
Nautical Mile	One minute of latitude; approximately 6,076 feet (1,852m) – about 1/8 longer than a statute mile of 5,280 feet
Neap Tides	The least tidal movement. This occurs twice a month when the moon is at a right angle to the sun; this happens on the moon's first and third quarters. When the combined gravitational pull of both the moon and the sun is the weakest this creates the lowest high water and the highest low water tides.
Port	The left side of a boat with bow in front (red light)
Reciprocal	After travelling from A to B, the opposite bearing to return from B to A
Screw	The boat's propeller
SMB	SMB is a buoy used by scuba divers, with a line, to indicate the diver's position to their surface safety boat. It is permanently inflated and carried throughout the dive.
Spring Tides	The greatest tidal movement. This occurs twice a month when the moon and the sun are in line; this happens on new and full moons. When the combined gravitational pull of both the moon and the sun is the strongest this creates the highest high water and the lowest low water tides.
Starboard	The right side of a boat with bow in front (green light)
Stern	The back area of the boat
Thermoclines	A layer of colder water sandwiched between the warmer well-mixed surface water layer and the colder denser lower layer. Seasonal thermoclines form layers in the shallower depths.
VLCC	Very large crude carrier

BIBLIOGRAPHY

Shipwrecks

- Dictionary of Disasters at Sea during the Age of Steam, by Charles Hocking (Lloyd's Register of Shipping, 1969)
- Hydrographic Department, Ministry of Defence, Taunton, Somerset TA12 2DN, United Kingdom. They provide an information service for commercial, private, Ministry of Defence and other government department enquiries. The wreck section has information on all post-1913 marine casualties occurring in continental shelf areas, except for American and Australian coastal waters. A search fee is charged.
- Information Group, Lloyd's Register of Shipping, 100 Leadenhall Street, London EC3A 3BP, United Kingdom. Brief ship details, date and place of losses recorded in quarterly returns, post 1890. This small specialist library also includes some books on shipwrecks. Open to the public.
- Last Hours of the Dara by PJ Abraham (Peter Davies, 1963)
- Lloyd's Marine Collection, Guildhall Library, Aldermanbury, London EC2P 2EJ, United Kingdom. Information on marine casualties and shipping movements worldwide from about 1740. Sources include Lloyd's List and war loss records. Open to the public.
- Modern Shipping Disasters 1963 – 1987 by Norman Hooke (Lloyd's of London Press, 1989)
- The Grey Widow-Maker by Bernard Edward (R Hale, 1990)

Marine Life

- Asia Pacific Reef Guide by Helmut Debelius (IKAN, available at Al Boom Diving)
- Coral Reef Animals of the Indo-Pacific by Terrence M Gosliner, David W Behrens & Gary C Williams (order from Sea Challengers, seachallengers.com)
- Coral Sea Reef Guide by Bob Halstead (available at Al Boom Diving)
- Coral Seas of Muscat (order from Sea Challengers, seachallengers.com)
- Indian Ocean Reef Guide by Helmut Debelius (IKAN, available at Al Boom Diving)
- Indo-Pacific Coral Reef Field Guide by Dr Gerald R Allen & Roger Steene (ISBN 981-00-5687-7, order from Sea Challengers, seachallengers.com)
- Nudibranchs & Sea Snails by Helmut Debelius (IKAN, available at Al Boom Diving)
- Red Sea Reef Guide by Helmut Debelius (Circle Books, available at Al Boom Diving)
- Reef Fishes UAE and Gulf of Oman by Richard F Field (Motivate Publishing)
- Seashells of Oman by Donald & Eloise Bosch (ISBN 0-582-78309-7, order online from Sea Challengers, seachallengers.com)
- The Coral Seas of Muscat by Frances Green & Richard Keech (ISBN 0-946510-28-8, order from Sea Challengers, seachallengers.com)

First Aid & Safety

- A Medical Guide to Hazardous Marine Life by Paul S Auerbach (Best Publishing, ISBN 0-941-33255-1)
- Red Sea Safety – Guide To Dangerous Marine Animals by Dr Peter Vine (Immel Publishing) (ISBN 0-907-15112-4)
- The Diving Emergency Handbook by John Lippmann & Stan Bugg (ISBN 0-946-02018-3)

DIRECTORY

Dive Companies & Dive Shops

West Coast

ABU DHABI

Abu Dhabi Sub Aqua Club
02 673 1111
the-club.com

Adventure Seekers
02 621 1811

Al Mahara Diving Center
02 643 7377
divemahara.com

Arabian Divers & Sportfishing Charters
050 6146 931
fishabudhabi.com

Desert Islands Watersport Centre
02 801 5454
desertislands.com

Emirates Divers Center
02 495 2013
emiratesdivers.com

Gulf Marine Sports
02 671 0017
gulfmarinesports.com

Nautica Environmental Associates
02 673 1250
nauticaenvironmental.com

Ocean Dive Center
02 644 1696
oceandivecenter.ae

Sea Hawk Water Sports
02 673 6688
shw-sports.com

AJMAN

Blue Planet Diving
050 1652 280
blue-planetdiving.com

DUBAI

Adventure HQ
04 346 6824
adventurehq.ae

Al Boom Diving
04 342 2993
alboomdiving.com

British Sub Aqua Club
055 4256 590
the-club.com

Emirates Diving Association
04 393 9390
emiratesdiving.com

Prodive Middle East
04 399 5711
prodiveme.com

Scubatec Diving Center
04 334 8988
scubatecdiving.com

Technical Diving International Center
04 393 0303
tdicenter.com

The Dive Centre
055 998 5806
thedivecentre.ae

The Dive Shop Dubai
04 813 5474
thediveshopdubai.com

The Pavilion Dive Centre
04 406 8828
jumeirah.com

RAS AL KHAIMAH

Adventure Divers
050 2914 479
adventuredivers.ae

Al Jazeera Diving & Swimming Center
07 244 5331
aljazeeradivecenter.com

SHARJAH

Emirates Diving Center
06 565 5990
emiratesdivingcentre.com

Sharjah Wanderers Dive Club
06 566 2105
sharjahwandererssc.com

East Coast

AL AQAH

Sandy Beach Diving Centre
09 244 5555
sandybm.com

Country code is +971 (UAE) and +968 (Oman)

DIBBA

Al Madhani Adventure Tourism
050 6905 080

Al Marsa Tours & Cargo
06 544 1232
almarsamusandam.com

Coastal Technical Divers
050 8696 707
coastaltechnicaldivers.com

Freestyle Divers
09 244 5756
freestyledivers.com

Nomad Ocean Adventures
02 683 6069
discovernomad.com

Scuba 2000
09 238 8477
scuba-2000.com

Sheesa Beach Travel and Tourism
02 683 6551
050 3336 046
sheesabeach.com

The Palms Dive Centre
09 204 3233
radissonblu.com

KHOR FAKKAN

7 Seas Divers
09 238 7400
7seasdivers.com

Divers Down UAE
09 237 0299
diversdownuae.com

Oceanic Diving Centre
09 238 5111
oceanichotel.com

Musandam

Extra Divers Musandam
02 673 0501
musandam-diving.com

Khasab Sea Tours
09 200 9440
kstoman.com

Khasab Travel & Tours
02 673 0464
khasabtours.com

Hotels & Resorts

West Coast

ABU DHABI

Beach Rotana ★★★★★
02 697 9000
rotana.com

Emirates Palace Hotel ★★★★★
02 690 9000
kempinski.com

Hilton Abu Dhabi ★★★★★
02 681 1900
hilton.com

InterContinental Abu Dhabi ★★★★★
02 666 6888
intercontinental.com

Le Royal Meridien Abu Dhabi ★★★★★
02 674 2020
leroyalmeridienabudhabi.com

Millennium Hotel Abu Dhabi ★★★★★
02 614 6000
millenniumhotels.com

Sheraton Abu Dhabi Hotel & Resort ★★★★★
02 677 3333
sheratonabudhabihotel.com

Sofitel Abu Dhabi Corniche ★★★★★
02 813 7777
sofitel.com

Golden Tulip Al Jazira Hotel & Resort ★★★★
02 562 9100
goldentulipaljazira.com

Al Ain Palace Hotel ★★★
02 679 4777
alainpalacehotel.com

Al Diar Capital Hotel ★★★
02 678 7700
aldiarhotels.com

Dhafra Beach Hotel ★★★
02 801 2000
danathotels.com

Al Diar Dana Hotel ★★
02 645 6000
aldiarhotels.com

AJMAN

Ajman Palace Hotel & Resort ★★★★★
06 701 8888
theajmanpalace.com

Ajman Saray ★★★★★
06 714 2222
ajmansaray.com

Kempinski Hotel Ajman (Has dive centre) ★★★★★
06 714 5555
kempinski.com

DUBAI

Al Qasr (Has dive centre) ★★★★★
04 366 8888
jumeirah.com

Burj Al Arab ★★★★★
04 301 7777
jumeirah.com

Dubai Marine Beach Resort & Spa ★★★★★
04 346 1111
dxbmarine.com

Habtoor Grand Beach Resort & Spa ★★★★★
04 399 5000
habtoorhotels.com

Hilton Dubai Jumeirah Resort ★★★★★
04 399 1111
hiltonhotelsmea.com

Hyatt Regency Dubai ★★★★★
04 209 1234
dubai.regency.hyatt.com

JA Jebel Ali Beach Hotel ★★★★★
04 883 6000
jaresortshotels.com

Jumeirah Beach Hotel (Has dive centre) ★★★★★
04 348 0000
jumeirah.com

Le Meridien Mina Seyahi Beach Resort & Marina ★★★★★
04 399 3333
lemeridien-minaseyahi.com

Mina A'Salam ★★★★★
04 366 8888
jumeirah.com

Ritz-Carlton Dubai Hotel ★★★★★
04 399 4000
ritzcarlton.com

Sheraton Jumeira Beach Resorts & Towers ★★★★★
04 399 5533
sheratonjumeirahbeach.com

Sofitel Dubai Palm Jumeirah Resort & Spa ★★★★★
04 455 6677
sofitel.com

The Palace At One&Only Royal Mirage ★★★★★
04 399 9999
oneandonlyroyalmirage.com

Westin Dubai Mina Seyahi Beach Resort & Marina ★★★★★
04 399 4141
westinminaseyahi.com

FUJAIRAH

Hilton Fujairah Resort ★★★★★
09 222 2411
hilton.com

Fortune Royal Hotel ★★★★
09 223 8886
fortunegroupofhotels.com

RAS AL KHAIMAH

Al Hamra Residence ★★★★★
07 206 7222
alhamraresorts.com

Banyan Tree Ras Al Khaimah Beach ★★★★★
07 206 7777
banyantree.com

DoubleTree by Hilton Resort & Spa Marjan Island ★★★★★
07 203 0000
doubletree3.hilton.com

Hilton Al Hamra Beach & Golf Resort ★★★★★
07 244 6666
hilton.com

Hilton Ras Al Khaimah ★★★★★
07 228 8888
hilton.com

Hilton Ras Al Khaimah Resort & Spa ★★★★★
07 228 8844
hilton.com

The Cove Rotana Resort ★★★★★
07 206 6000
rotana.com

Waldorf Astoria Ras Al Khaimah ★★★★★
07 203 5555
waldorfastoria3.hilton.com

Bin Majid Beach Resort ★★★★
07 244 6644
binmajid.com

Sells dive gear Has dive centre Country code is +971 (UAE) and +968 (Oman)

Golden Tulip Khatt Springs Resort & Spa ★★★★
07 244 8777
goldentulipkhattsprings.com

Ras Al Khaimah Hotel ★★★★
07 236 2999
fivecontinentsgroup.com

RUWAIS

Dhafra Beach Hotel ★★★
02 801 2000
danathotels.com

SHARJAH

Radisson Blu Resort Sharjah ★★★★★
06 565 7777
radissonblu.com

Royal Beach Resort & Spa ★★★★★
06 536 5550
royalbeachresortspa.com

Coral Beach Resort ★★★★
06 522 9999
coral-beachresortsharjah.com

Holiday International Sharjah ★★★★
06 573 6666
holidayinternational.com

Sharjah Grand Hotel ★★★★
06 528 5557
sharjahgrand.com

Lou Lou'a Beach Resort ★★★
06 528 5000
loulouabeach.com

UMM AL QUWAIN

Palma Beach Resort ★★★★
06 766 7090
palmagroup.ae

Pearl Hotel ★★★★
06 766 6678
pearlhotel.ae

Umm Al Quwain Beach Hotel ★★★★
06 766 6647
ummalquwainbeachotel.com

Barracuda Beach Resort ★★★
06 768 1555
barracuda.ae

Flamingo Beach Resort ★★★
06 765 0000
flamingoresort.ae

East Coast

AL AQAH

Fujairah Rotana Resort & Spa - Al Aqah Beach ★★★★★
09 244 9888
rotana.com

Iberotel Miramar Al Aqah Beach Resort ★★★★★
09 244 9994
iberotel.com

Le Meridien Al Aqah Beach Resort ★★★★★
09 244 9000
lemeridien-alaqah.com

Fujairah Beach Motel ★★★★
09 222 8111

Royal Beach Hotel & Resort ★★★★
09 244 9444
royalbeach.ae

Sandy Beach Hotel & Resort ★★★★
09 244 5555
sandybm.com

DIBBA OMAN

Nomad Ocean Adventures (The Eco Lodge)
050 885 3238 / 02 683 6069
discovernomad.com

DIBBA UAE

Radisson Blu Resort Fujairah ★★★★★
09 244 9700
radissonblu.com

Holiday Beach Motel ★★★
09 244 5540
holidaybeachmotel.com

KHOR FAKKAN

Oceanic Resort & Spa ★★★★
09 238 5111
oceanichotel.com

Oman

MUSSANAH

Millennium Resort Mussanah ★★★★
268 71555
millenniumhotels.com

DIRECTORY FURTHER INFO

INDEX

Explorer Products

Residents' Guides

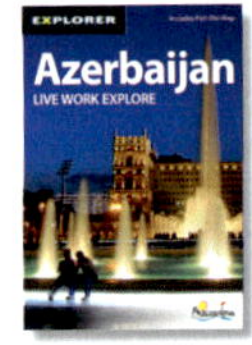

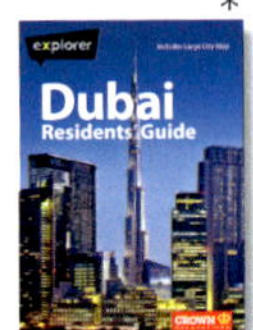

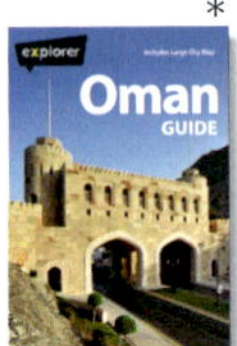

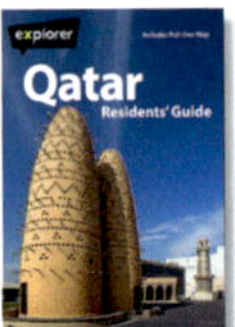

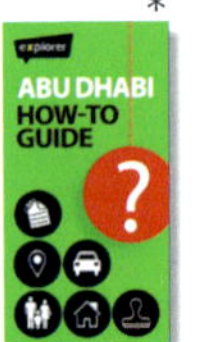

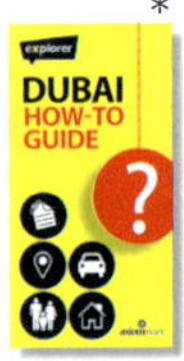

Visitors' Guides

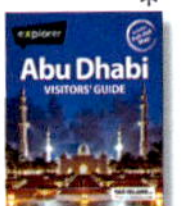

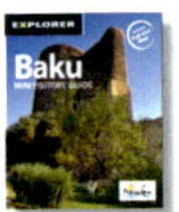

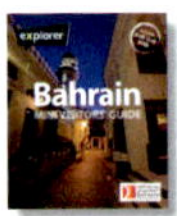

Photography Books & Calendars

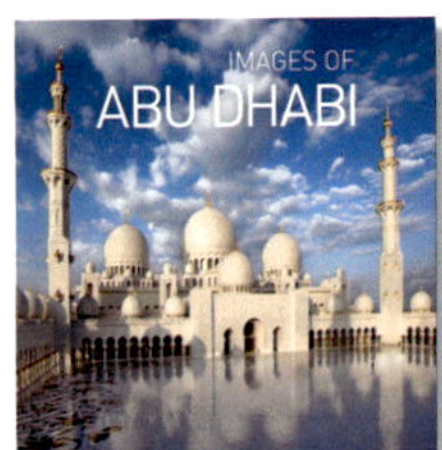

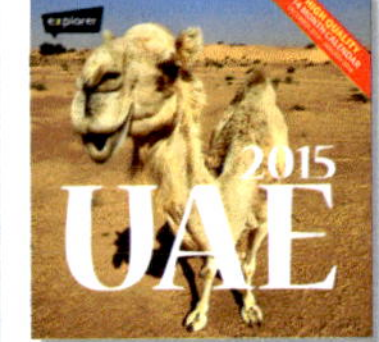

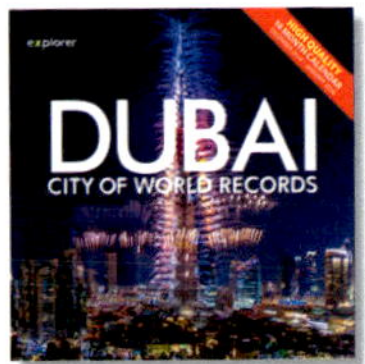

Check out ask**explorer**.com

Maps

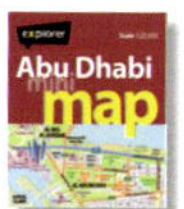
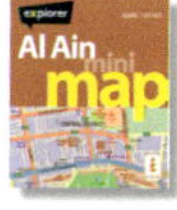

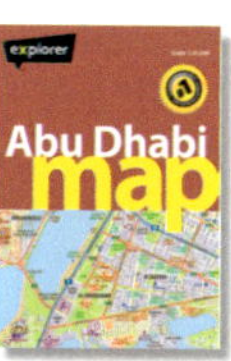

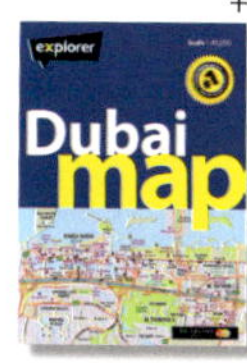

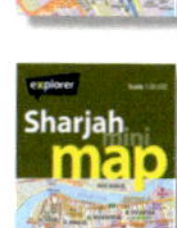

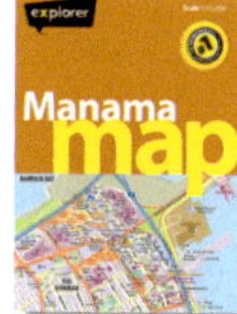
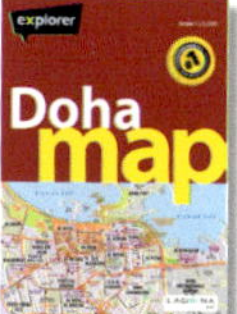
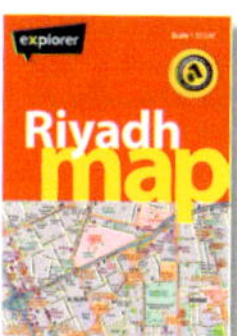
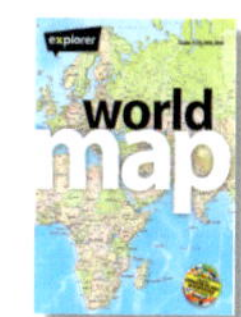
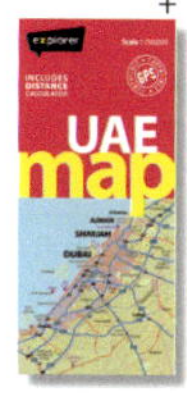

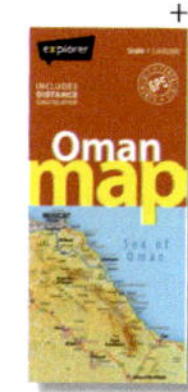
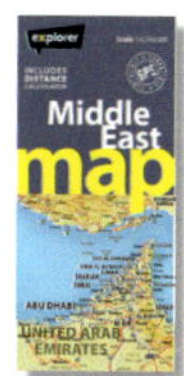

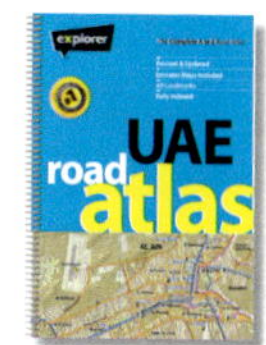

Adventure & Lifestyle Guides

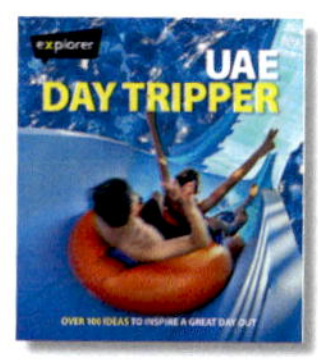
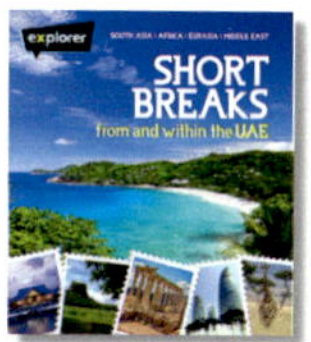
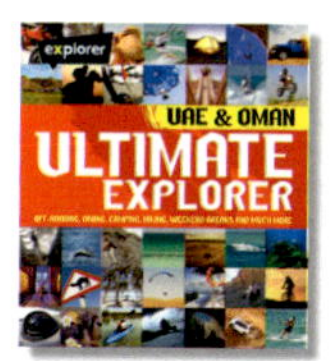
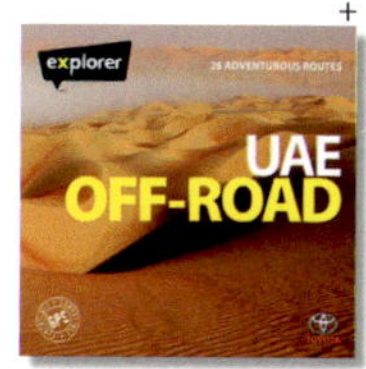

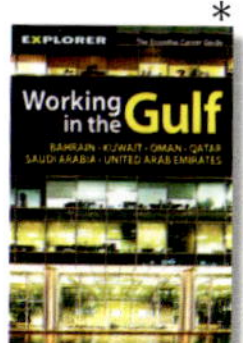
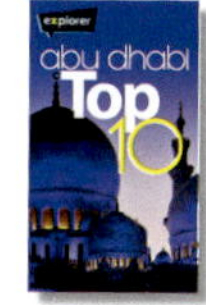

Apps & eBooks

+ Also available as applications. Visit askexplorer.com/apps.

* Now available in eBook format.

Visit askexplorer.com/shop.

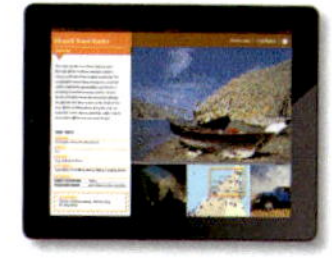

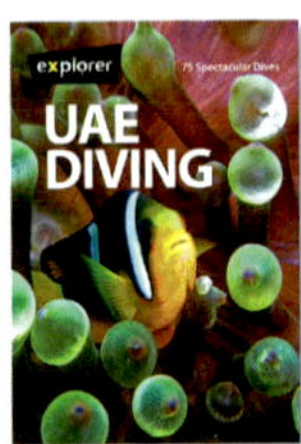

UAE Diving – 4th edition

Lead Editor Kirsty Tuxford
Proofread by Lidiya Baltova-Kalichuk, Fiona MacKenzie
Data managed by Mimi Stankova
Designed by Ieyad Charaf, Mohammed Shakkeer
Maps by Zain Madathil, Dhanya Nellikkunnummal
Photographs (2014) by Francis Leguen, Abdullah Al Meheiri, Shamsa Al Hameli
Special thanks to the following people for their invaluable input, time, expertise and knowledge – without them we would not have been able to write or illustrate this book: Ali Fikree, Bill Leeman, Brian Davies, British Sub Aqua Club 1339/Desert Sports Diving Club, Christine Schroder, Eric Laing and Capt. Joe Finch at Inchcape Shipping Services, Guy Ploegaerts, John Gregory, John Tilley, Kurt Luedi of Maku Dive Center, Leon Betts, Maps Geosystems, Paul Algate at Scuba International, Paul Sant at Divers Down, Phil Holt, Phil O'Shea at Pavillon Dive Centre, Seraj Alali at White Sea Shipping, Stephanie Davies at Scuba Dubai, Stevie Macleod at Scuba Dubai, Stuart Scott Ely and Terry Day.

Publishing
Chief Content Officer & Founder Alistair MacKenzie

Editorial
Managing Editor Carli Allan
Editors Kirsty Tuxford, Lily Lawes, Lisa Crowther
Research Manager Mimi Stankova
Researchers Amrit Raj, Roja P, Praseena, Shalu Sukumar, Maria Luisa Reyes, Lara Santizo, Jayleen Aguinaldo, Jacqueline Reyes, Yuliya Molchanova

Design & Photography
Art Director Ieyad Charaf
Layout Manager Jayde Fernandes
Junior Designer Mohammed Shakkeer
Cartography Manager Zain Madathil
Cartographers Noushad Madathil, Dhanya Nellikkunnummal, Ramla Kambravan, Jithesh Kalathingal, Jobydas KD
GIS Analyst Joby Das
Photographer & Image Editor Hardy Mendrofa

Sales & Marketing
Director of Sales Peter Saxby
Media Sales Area Managers Laura Zuffova, Sabrina Ahmed, Bryan Anes, Louise Burton, Simon Reddy
Digital Sales Manager Rola Touffaha
Business Development Manager Pouneh Hafizi
Director of Retail Ivan Rodrigues
Retail Sales Coordinator Michelle Mascarenhas
Retail Sales Area Supervisors Ahmed Mainodin, Firos Khan
Retail Sales Merchandisers Johny Mathew, Shan Kumar, Mehmood Ullah
Retail Sales Drivers Shabsir Madathil, Nimicias Arachchige
Warehouse Assistant Mohamed Haji, Jithinraj M

Finance, HR & Administration
Accountant Cherry Enriquez
Accounts Assistants Sunil Suvarna, Jeanette Enecillo
Administrative Assistant Joy H. San Buenaventura
Reception Jayfee Manseguiao
Public Relations Officer Rafi Jamal
Office Assistant Shafeer Ahamed
Office Manager – India Jithesh Kalathingal

IT & Digital Solutions
Web Developer Mirza Ali Nasrullah, Waqas Razzaq
HTML/UI Developer Naveed Ahmed
IT Manager R. Ajay
Database Programmer Pradeep T.P.

Contact Us

General Enquiries
We'd love to hear your thoughts and answer any questions you have about this book or any other Explorer product. Contact us at **info@askexplorer.com**

Careers
If you fancy yourself as an Explorer, send your CV (stating the position you're interested in) to **jobs@askexplorer.com**

Contract Publishing
For enquiries about Explorer's Contract Publishing arm and design services contact **contracts@askexplorer.com**

Retail Sales
Our products are available in most good bookshops as well as online at askexplorer.com/shop.
retail@askexplorer.com

PR & Marketing
For PR and marketing enquiries contact **marketing@askexplorer.com**

Corporate Sales & Licensing
For bulk sales and customisation options, as well as licensing of this book or any Explorer product, contact **leads@askexplorer.com**

Advertising & Sponsorship
For advertising and sponsorship, contact **sales@askexplorer.com**

Explorer Publishing & Distribution
PO Box 34275, Dubai, United Arab Emirates
askexplorer.com

Phone: +971 (0)4 340 8805
Fax: +971 (0)4 340 8806